# Walking Weekends

## *Peak District*

*Mark Reid*

*24 circular walks from 12 villages*
*throughout the Peak District,*
*with two walks of varying lengths*
*from each village – ideal for a weekend break.*

InnWay Publications

# Walking Weekends
## Peak District

*Published by:*
INNWAY PUBLICATIONS
102 LEEDS ROAD
HARROGATE
HG2 8HB

ISBN: 978-1-902001-12-8

This book is dedicated to Elvis, my German Shorthaired Pointer
*...who accompanied me on every walk.*

Thank you to Rachel Gospel, Ian Belcher, Anthony Cake,
Bernadette and Stewart Reid for accompanying me on
many of the walks.

Front cover photograph: Froggatt Edge
Back cover photograph: Upper Sett Valley
4-page colour insert photographs
© Mark Reid 2006

Illustrations © John A. Ives, Dringhouses, York.
www.johnaives.co.uk

Typeset, printed and bound by Spectrum Print, Cleethorpes.

# CONTENTS

Walking Weekend 8   **Hayfield**        129

*Saturday walk - Edale Cross, Kinder Downfall & Snake Path*      10.5 miles

*Sunday walk - The Sett Valley Trail, Lantern Pike & Little Hayfield*      5.5 miles

---

Walking Weekend 9   **Longnor**        147

*Saturday walk - Shining Ford, Manifold Head, Flash & Dove Head*      11.5 miles

*Sunday walk - Earl Sterndale, Chrome Hill & Hollinsclough*      8.5 miles

---

Walking Weekend 10   **Tideswell**        165

*Saturday walk - Litton Mill, Brushfield, Monsal Viaduct & Cressbrook Dale*      9.75 miles

*Sunday walk - Monk's Dale, Wormhill, Chee Dale & Miller's Dale Station*      8.5 miles

---

Walking Weekend 11   **Wetton**        182

*Saturday walk - The Manifold Valley, Ilam, Dovedale & Hopedale*      9.5 miles

*Sunday walk - Ecton Hill, Manifold Way, Wetton Mill & Thor's Cave*      6.5 miles

---

Walking Weekend 12   **Youlgrave**        199

*Saturday walk - Lathkill Dale, Monyash, Cales Dale & Bradford Dale*      11.5 miles

*Sunday walk - Robin Hood's Stride, Nine Ladies Stone Circle & Stanton in Peak*      8 miles

---

GREATER
MANCHESTER

DARK
PEAK

SHEFFIELD

HAYFIELD
EDALE

RIVER
SETT

CASTLETON

HATHERSAGE

TIDESWELL

EYAM

BASLOW

RIVER WYE

BAKEWELL

RIVER
DERWENT

LONGNOR

YOULGRAVE

RIVER
MANIFOLD

HARTINGTON

WHITE

WETTON

RIVER
DOVE

PEAK

# INTRODUCTION

Picture the scene: it is late October and the light is beginning to fade as you head down from the wilds of Kinder Scout towards Grindsbrook Booth in the heart of the Vale of Edale with its cluster of houses, twinkling lights and rising smoke. Contentedly tired, you lift the door-latch of the Old Nag's Head and walk into the warmth of the bar with its convivial chatter and glowing fire in the grate; you have earned this food and drink. You have time to relax, recuperate and recall the day's adventures before retiring to your comfortable bed, ready for the next day. The village pub is as much a part of the Peak District as the gritstone moors, the irreplaceable hub of rural life where you can experience the delightful regional nuances that makes Britain so special; local accents, customs, food and drink. This is something to be experienced, not read about – in fact, writing about it makes me want to get out there and live it, carefully planned of course to finish at a good pub!

What makes the Peak District so special is the varied and contrasting landscape within such a compact area. Broadly defined by its underlying rocks, the Peak District is divided into the Dark and White Peak. The White Peak forms the central and southern part of the Peak District and is characterised by a high limestone plateau that is criss-crossed by a myriad of drystone walls where you will find attractive villages and cosy pubs. This plateau is dissected by incredibly deep and steep-sided valleys cloaked in ancient woodland through which flow crystal-clear streams. The Dark Peak surrounds this limestone plateau to the west, north and east and is a world of broad valleys, jagged escarpments and windswept moorland that has a wild, untamed feel about it. Bring these two together in close proximity and you have some of the best walking country in the world. Add to this a fascinating history literally beneath every footstep, from mystical stone circles to the splendour of Chatsworth House, and a walk through the Peak District becomes a memorable experience.

By spending a weekend in the Peak District staying, eating, drinking and walking locally, you can forget about carbon footprints, as the only footprints you will leave behind will be muddy ones!

Mark Reid, *October 2006*

# ROUTE DESCRIPTIONS & MAPS

## ROUTE DESCRIPTIONS

The following abbreviations have been used throughout the route descriptions:

| | | | |
|---|---|---|---|
| SP | Signpost | BW | Bridleway |
| FP | Footpath | FB | Footbridge |

The detailed route descriptions and hand-drawn maps should guide you safely around the routes featured in this book. However, always take Ordnance Survey Explorer maps (scale 1:25,000) with you on your walks, as well as a compass or GPS. The countryside is slowly but constantly evolving and changing; stiles may become bridle-gates, gates may disappear, paths may be re-surfaced, pubs or shops may close. Occasionally, Rights of Way may be altered or diverted to prevent erosion damage or to improve the line of the footpath. Any changes will be clearly signposted and must be followed, and are usually marked on the most up-to-date Ordnance Survey maps.

Footpaths and bridleways throughout the Peak District National Park are generally well maintained with good waymarking. The signposts are often colour-coded as follows: yellow for footpaths, blue for bridleways and red for byways. Often, the path on the ground is clearly defined and easy to follow, however, some sections cross remote areas and high moorland where route finding may be difficult, especially in bad weather.

## MAPS

The following Ordnance Survey Explorer maps (1:25,000) cover the walks featured in this book.

OL1 *'The Peak District Dark Peak area'.* This map covers Hayfield, Kinder Scout, Edale, Castleton, Hope Valley, Ladybower Reservoir, Hathersage and the Upper Derwent Valley.

OL24 *'The Peak District White Peak area'.* This map covers Eyam, Tideswell, Monsal Dale, Bakewell, Baslow, Chatsworth Park, Youlgrave, Lathkill Dale, Hartington, Wetton, Longnor, Dovedale and the Manifold Valley.

# SAFETY

Never underestimate the strenuous nature of walking particularly when this is combined with high ground and the elements. Do not attempt to complete a walk that is beyond your skill, experience or level of fitness.

Obtain a detailed weather forecast before setting out on your walk. If the weather turns bad then turn back the way you have walked. Conditions can change for the worse within minutes making walking hazardous with mist, winds and rain virtually all year round. The weather conditions on moorland can vary significantly from conditions in valleys.

Take Ordnance Survey maps (1:25,000) of the area as well as a GPS (Global Positioning System) or compass.

Your boots are the most important thing; make sure that they are waterproof, comfortable and have good ankle support and sturdy soles.

Waterproof and windproof coat and trousers are essential as well as gloves, hat and fleece for warmth. Travel light as a heavy rucksack can tire you out. Take essential items such as a fleece, snack food, first aid kit, blister plasters, sun cream, whistle, water bottle, torch and 'survival' bag. Drink plenty of fluids (not alcohol) and eat food regularly to keep energy levels up.

Always walk in a group unless you are very experienced and inform someone of your intended route and report your safe arrival. In an emergency summon help with six blasts of your whistle or call the Police (who will contact the Mountain Rescue Team) giving details of the incident and location.

Take care when crossing rivers or roads and walk in single file (facing oncoming traffic) when walking along country lanes. Do not explore old mine or quarry workings.

When walking through grassy moorland keep a watchful eye for adders, Britain's only poisonous snake. If bitten, seek medical help immediately.

Above all, keep your hands out of your pockets and look where you are going! *REMEMBER: "An experienced walker knows when to turn back"*

# COUNTRYSIDE CODE

### Consider other people
*Showing consideration and respect for other people makes the countryside a pleasant environment for everyone – at home, at work and at leisure.*

### Enjoy the countryside and respect its life and work
*We have a responsibility to protect our countryside now and for future generation. Tread gently – discover the beauty of the natural environment and take care not to damage, destroy or remove features such as rocks, plants and trees. Do not touch crops, machinery or livestock.*

### Leave gates and property as you find them
*Please respect the working life of the countryside, as our actions can affect people's livelihoods, our heritage, and the safety and welfare of animals and ourselves. Use stiles and gates to cross fences and walls and close gates behind you.*

### Keep to public Rights of Way or Open Access areas.
*Footpaths are for walkers; bridleways are for cyclists, horse-riders and walkers. Motorbikes and cars should keep to roads.*

### Do not make excessive noise
*The hills and valleys should be quiet places*

### Safeguard water supplies
*Streams are used by livestock and often feed reservoirs for drinking supplies.*

### Guard against risk of fire
*Uncontrolled fires can devastate grassy hillsides or moorland.*

### Keep dogs under control
*A loose dog can be catastrophic for ground nesting birds, sheep and sometimes the dog itself. By law, farmers are entitled to destroy a dog that injures or worries their animals.*

### Take litter home
*Litter is dangerous and unsightly.*

### Safety
*Weather can change quickly, are you fully equipped for the hills?*

# BAKEWELL

*Bakewell can trace its history back to Saxon times when King Edward the Elder built a fort on a hill overlooking the River Wye in 924AD. The Normans later built a motte and bailey castle on this site to guard the important river crossing, now known as Castle Hill. During this time an important church was founded on the hillside to the west of the river; this Saxon settlement was known as Badequella, or 'bath well', after the numerous springs that rose in the area. A wealth of artefacts remain from this period including two Saxon preaching crosses and a large collection of carved stones. All Saints Church stands on the site of this Saxon church, its octagonal tower and sharp spire rising high above the rooftops. It dates mainly from the 13th and 14th Centuries, although heavily restored in Victorian times, and is noted for its many fine monuments, particularly in the Vernon Chapel. By the early 14th Century, Bakewell had been granted a charter to hold weekly markets and annual fairs, which are still held to this day. During the late 17th Century the Duke of Rutland decided to develop Bakewell as a spa town to rival nearby Buxton and built a Bath House above a chalybeate spring in the town centre. This was short-lived as the spa was not as popular as the warmer waters of Buxton but it did herald a period of prosperity for Bakewell. There are several historic buildings around All Saints Church including the Old Town Hall and Almshouses of St John's Hospital along King Street, both of which were built in 1709. In the town centre you will find the Old Original Bakewell Pudding Shop that still makes Bakewell Puddings (not tarts!) from the original recipe. This famous delicacy was inadvertently invented during the 1850's at the Rutland Arms when the cook poured the pastry mix over the jam instead of the other way round!*

## THE VILLAGE

Bakewell is a thriving town and offers several pubs, hotels, Youth Hostel, cafés, restaurants, bakeries, a variety of traditional shops, large supermarket, gift and craft shops, outdoor retailers, chemist, a bookshop, several High Street banks, the Old Original Bakewell Pudding Shop, Tourist Information Centre and a weekly street market (Monday).

## ACCOMMODATION

Tourist Information Centre, Bakewell:     01629 816558

## BAKEWELL PUBS

**Castle Inn, Bakewell:**                **01629 812103**

This 300 year old coaching inn is situated near the historic bridge across the Wye. Inside, it has plenty of character with stone-flagged floors and a cosy corner with wooden settles around an open fire set in a stone hearth. Steps lead down to a dining room with old beams and another large fireplace.

**The Manners, Bakewell:**               **01629 812756**

Just out of the town centre along Haddon Road, this friendly town pub was originally called the Vernon Arms but changed its name to The Manners when Robinson's Brewery bought it back in 1920.

**Peacock, Bakewell:**                   **01629 812994**

Situated behind the historic Market Hall, this traditional pub boasts several comfortable rooms as well as a very cosy snug. Outside, its attractive stone frontage is often adorned with flower baskets.

**Queens Arms, Bakewell:**               **01629 814586**

Adjacent to the Peacock, the Queens Arms has a more contemporary feel with floorboards and comfy sofas as well as a separate pool room.

**Red Lion, Bakewell:**                  **01629 812054**

This low, attractive pub dates back to the 17th Century when it was a coaching inn. Today, it offers a traditional bar with a stone-flagged floor and lovely stone fireplace as well as a comfortable lounge and separate dining room.

**Rutland Arms Hotel, Bakewell:**       **01629 812812**

Built in 1804 on the site of the old White Horse Inn, this elegant late Georgian coaching inn retains many original features including a sweeping staircase, hob-grate fireplaces and lots of grandfather clocks quietly ticking away. Over the years, the Rutland Arms has welcomed many famous guests including Turner, Byron, Coleridge, Wordsworth and Jane Austen, who based the town of Lambton on Bakewell in her book 'Pride and Prejudice'.

**Wheatsheaf, Bakewell:**       **01629 812985**

This large, busy pub has an open plan interior served by a central bar with lots of drinking/dining areas, as well as a separate large dining room to the rear.

## PUBS ALONG THE WALKS

| | |
|---|---|
| Devonshire Arms, Beeley: | 01629 733259 |
| Peacock, Rowsley: | 01629 733518 |
| Grouse & Claret, Rowsley: | 01629 733233 |
| Packhorse Inn, Little Longstone: | 01629 640471 |
| Stables Bar, Monsal Head: | 01629 640250 |
| Ashford Arms, Ashford in the Water: | 01629 812725 |
| Bull's Head, Ashford in the Water: | 01629 812931 |

# Bakewell Walking Weekend
# - Saturday Walk -

*Bakewell, Calton Pastures, Chatsworth Park,*
*Rowsley & the River Wye.*

## WALK INFORMATION

| | |
|---|---|
| Highlights | The Russian Cottage, a mill caught in a storm, Chatsworth deer park, beautiful estate villages, a marooned station and England's finest medieval hall. |
| Distance | 10 miles          Time          4 - 5 hours |
| Maps | OS Explorer OL24 |
| Refreshments | Pubs, shops and/or cafés at Bakewell, Beeley and Rowsley. Café at Calton Lees. |
| Terrain | Mixture of woodland, field and riverside paths with long stretches along clear stony/muddy tracks. The section alongside the River Wye may be boggy underfoot. |
| Ascents | Calton Pastures - 266 metres above sea level. |
| Caution | There is a steep climb up through Manners Wood. The riverside path from Haddon Park to Bakewell may be impassable after heavy rain; an alternative route has been included. Take care crossing the road at Calton Lees, Beeley and Rowsley. |

This walk explores the undulating hills to the east of Bakewell between the Wye and Derwent rivers, taking in the estates of the dukes of Devonshire and Rutland. After a brisk climb up through Manners Wood, a broad sweep of hillside opens out before you known as Calton Pastures, from where there are far-reaching views across the Derwent Valley. A delightful path leads down to reach the hamlet of Calton Houses hidden at the head of a wooded side-valley, from where it is easy walking all the way to Calton Lees and the southern edge of Chatsworth Park. This vast swathe of parkland surrounds Chatsworth House, home of the Duke of Devonshire, and once formed the western edge of Sherwood Forest, although the present park was largely created by the 4th Duke during the mid 18th Century with the help of 'Capability' Brown. The derelict mill and One Arch Bridge at the southern end of the park were designed by James Paine who also designed the Stables at Chatsworth House during the 1760's. This corn mill worked until 1952, but was partly destroyed during a gale in 1962.

Beeley has been an estate village of the Dukes of Devonshire since the mid 18th Century when it was purchased as part of the 'grand plan' to redevelop Chatsworth Park. St Anne's Church dates back to Norman times, although only fragments remain of this early church as it was heavily restored in the 1880's. Many of the houses throughout the village date from a building spree during the 19th Century by the 6th Duke, but some older properties remain including the 17th Century Old Hall and the 18th Century Devonshire Arms. This classic Peakland pub was once a coaching inn that welcomed many famous customers including Charles Dickens and King Edward VII, who supposedly met his mistress Alice Keppel here! Although a number of properties are now privately owned, the blue livery of the Chatsworth Estate is still in evidence.

Rowsley is situated at the confluence of the rivers Wye and Derwent on the edge of the National Park boundary. It is a village divided by the River Derwent, which is spanned by a 15th Century packhorse bridge that has been widened several times. The settlement on the eastern riverbank, once known as Little Rowsley, developed following the arrival of the Midland Railway's line from Derby in 1849. The railway terminated at Rowsley until 1863 because the Duke of Devonshire did not want it to cross Chatsworth Park. An alternative route was found up through the Wye Valley across the Duke of Rutland's estate on condition that it was concealed in deep cuttings and tunnels as it passed Haddon Hall. The only problem was that the original Rowsley Station, designed by Joseph Paxton, was now sited in the wrong place as it had been built for the proposed Derwent Valley route. Paxton's station was left marooned and demoted to use as sidings and yards whilst a new station was built just to the south. When the railway closed in 1968 between Matlock and Buxton the old railway yards were redeveloped as the Peak Village shopping centre with Paxton's station as its centrepiece. To the west of the riverbank lies Great Rowsley, the original settlement that has a real village atmosphere with its water fountain, farms, cottages and St Katherine's Church. The most impressive building is the Peacock, built in 1652 as a yeoman's house on land leased from the Manners family of Haddon Hall who also held the manor of Rowsley and whose crest features a peacock. For a time the building was used as the dower house of Haddon Hall but has been an inn since the 1820's.

An old lane climbs out of Rowsley skirting across the wooded hillside before crossing Haddon Park to join the banks of the River Wye. Out of sight along this walk, but only a short detour away, is Haddon Hall, the Derbyshire home of the Duke of Rutland. This hall dates back to the 12th Century when it was the home of the Vernon family, who had come over to England with William the Conqueror. They held it until the 16th Century when it passed to the Manners family following the marriage of Dorothy Vernon to Sir John Manners, son of the Earl of Rutland. They subsequently became the Dukes of Rutland and spent much of their time at Belvoir Castle in Leicestershire especially during the 18th and 19th Centuries, thus leaving Haddon Hall untouched for two centuries. Haddon Hall is one of the finest medieval manor houses in England.

*For more information about Chatsworth House & Park,*
*see Walking Weekend 2.*

# BAKEWELL SATURDAY WALK

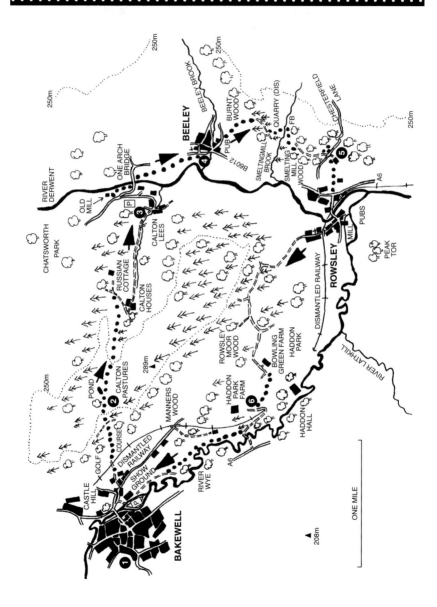

17

# THE WALK

*1.* From the roundabout in the centre of Bakewell (with your back to the Rutland Arms), walk down through the town centre along Bridge Street to reach the ancient bridge across the River Wye, after which turn right along Station Road and right again along Coombs Road. Follow this road straight on then, where the houses end on your right, turn left through a gate (SP) and up along a driveway to reach a fork in the lane near some houses. Head up to the right through a gate then, where this lane bends to the left after a short distance, carry straight on up across the field alongside the wall to reach a bridge across the disused railway line (Monsal Trail). After the bridge, follow the path up across the golf course *(beware of golf balls)* into Manners Wood. Head up through the woods, bending up to the right to reach a fork in the path beside a small stream where you follow the left-hand path climbing quite steeply up to soon join a rough track across your path. Turn right then immediately left after the small stream along a rough path climbing steeply up to reach a wall-gate at the top of the woods.

*2.* After the wall-gate, bear right across the middle of the field passing to the right of an enclosed copse of woodland to reach a stile beside a pond. Cross the stile then head left over another stile beside a gate, after which turn right and follow the indistinct grassy path gradually bearing away from the fence heading down across the large field to reach a gate in a fence at the bottom of the field just to the left of Calton Plantation. Head through the gate and follow the grassy track straight on down to reach a junction of tracks just before a large barn *(quaint 'Russian Cottage' just ahead)*. At this junction, turn right back on yourself slightly and follow this track on to join a wall on your left (above a wooded valley) which you follow down to reach a gate in the bottom field corner. Head through the gate and follow the track down to the left to reach the cottages at Calton Houses. Follow the track between the houses, winding sharply down to the valley floor then carry on along the track heading down the valley for 0.75 miles to reach a junction of lanes and tracks on the edge of Calton Lees.

3. At this junction, head straight on along the metalled lane and follow this curving round to the left to reach the parking area beside Chatsworth Garden Centre. Carry straight on through the parking area to join the main road through Chatsworth Park beside a cattle grid. Cross the road just beyond the cattle grid then drop down to the right across Chatsworth Park to join the banks of the River Derwent near the derelict mill. Follow the path to the right downstream to join the road beside One Arch Bridge across the River Derwent. Turn left over the bridge then immediately right through a kissing-gate (SP) and follow the path, flanked with trees, straight on to re-join the road opposite Beeley Church.

4. Cross the road and follow the lane opposite passing St Anne's Church on your left up into Beeley then, at the junction just after the Church, turn right then right again down to reach the Devonshire Arms. Pass in front of the pub then turn left immediately after it and follow the road up out of the village leaving the houses behind then take the FP to the right through a small gate in the hedge (SP). Head straight on alongside the fence on your right and through a gate, after which turn left up alongside the fence on your left to reach a squeeze-stile at the top of the field. After the stile, bear right up through another squeeze-stile in a wall, after which slant up across the hillside to join a track that leads to a gate on the edge of Burnt Wood. Head into the woods then, after a few paces, follow the right-hand level path heading through the woods then, where the path forks again after 150 yards, follow the left-hand narrow path heading straight on through the trees to soon join a wide path which you follow up to the left through a gap in a large retaining wall set in a disused quarry. Follow the path straight on to soon reach a FB to your right over Smeltingmill Brook, after which follow the path gently dropping down with the wooded ravine to your right at first then bearing left through the woods up to join a track across your path. Turn right along this track and follow it through the woods then, where it bends down to the right to a gate at the end of the woods that leads onto a road (Chesterfield Lane), branch off to the left through the woods to quickly reach a bridlegate in a fence (Toll

Bar Cottage just ahead). Head through the bridlegate and walk straight across the garden skirting behind the house and through a gate that leads onto the road (Chesterfield Lane).

5. Turn right down along the road passing in front of Toll Bar Cottage just beyond which (after the entrance to Woodside), take the FP to the left through a squeeze-stile (SP 'Rowsley'). Follow this path straight on down across the hillside, enclosed for most of the way, to join the main A6 road at Rowsley. Turn right along the A6 towards 'Buxton, Manchester', over the bridge across the Derwent then turn right along Church Lane immediately after the Peacock. Follow this road up until you reach the last house on your left at the end of the metalled lane. Carry straight on along the enclosed track climbing steadily up for 0.5 miles until you come to a barrier across the track on the edge of Rowsleymoor Wood. After this barrier, follow the track to the left then straight on through the woods, level at first then gently rising up to emerge from the woods (ignore track up to right) where you carry straight on gently dropping down to reach a T-junction with another track. Turn left along the track to soon reach a fork where you bear right towards 'Bakewell'. Follow this track straight on then curving down to the left passing the entrance to Bowling Green Farm just after which, where the track bends sharp right, carry straight on along the BW down to quickly reach a gate to your right that leads out onto a field. Walk straight on alongside the fence on your left across fields then bending down to the left to join a lane (Haddon Park Farm across to your right).

6. Turn left along the lane and follow this lane winding down then, where the lane levels out as you approach the bridge across the River Wye, turn right through a bridlegate beside a gate (SP) *. After the bridlegate, follow the path straight on keeping close to the field boundary and wooded riverside on your left to reach a (second) markerpost after 400 yards (ignore BW off to the right) where you carry straight on down some steps then along the riverside to reach a stile that leads onto the wooded riverbank. Follow the riverside path straight on and cross a small FB that leads out onto a field. Carry straight on across the field alongside the hedge on your right passing

a meander in the river just after which, at a gate and small bridge in this hedge, bear slightly away from the hedge cutting off the field corner to re-join the hedge on your right. Follow this hedge straight on across Bakewell Showground to reach a cattle grid and a junction of roads beside the Show Office, where you follow the riverside path to the left and cross the second FB across the Wye that leads back into Bakewell.

*Alternative route if riverside path flooded: After the bridlegate, follow the path straight on keeping close to the field boundary and wooded riverside on your left to reach a (second) markerpost after 400 yards. Follow the BW ahead bearing gradually up to the right across the field to reach a bridlegate in a fence that leads onto a track along the bottom edge of woodland. Turn left along this track and follow it to join a metalled lane beside an old railway viaduct. Turn left along this lane (Coombs Road) and follow it back into Bakewell.*

Bakewell

# Bakewell Walking Weekend
## - Sunday Walk -
### Bakewell, Monsal Trail, Little Longstone & Ashford in the Water

## WALK INFORMATION

Highlights     Full steam ahead along the Monsal Trail, classic Peakland pubs, a famous viewpoint, a controversial viaduct, Sheepwash Bridge and one of the prettiest villages in the Peak District.

Distance     8 miles        Time        3 hours

Maps     OS Explorer OL24

Refreshments     Pubs, shops and/or cafés at Bakewell, Monsal Head and Ashford in the Water. Pub at Little Longstone.

Terrain     From Bakewell, this walk follows a stony/grassy track up out of the Wye valley to join the track-bed of the former Midland Railway (Monsal Trail). This cinder track-bed is followed for 1.25 miles before field paths cut off to Little Longstone. After a short section of road walking, a narrow path traverses the steep wooded slopes above Monsal Dale before joining an old track that leads down into Ashford. Riverside and woodland paths lead back to Bakewell.

Ascents     Monsal Head - 270 metres above sea level.

Caution     There are steep drops to the side of the path above Monsal Dale. Take care crossing the road at Monsal Head and on the outskirts of Bakewell.

# POINTS OF INTEREST

From its source on Axe Edge just to the south of Buxton, the infant River Wye flows eastwards through Buxton skirting huge quarries before cutting a deep swathe through the White Peak limestone plateau. The character of the valley changes constantly, reflected by its numerous name changes including Chee Dale, Miller's Dale, Water-cum-Jolly Dale and finally Monsal Dale. This is a landscape of gleaming limestone scars, deep wooded valleys, attractive villages and cosy pubs. At Ashford in the Water, the Wye leaves the limestone gorges behind and meanders through a broader valley of rich pastures and woodland copse to swell the Derwent at Rowsley. At Bakewell, the river flows beneath a wonderful 13th Century bridge that still carries the main road into the town. Just upstream is Holme Bridge, a superb example of a packhorse bridge that was built in 1664 to replace an earlier bridge. This narrow, low slung bridge was designed to allow fully laden packhorses to cross unhindered and was an important river crossing along a busy packhorse route; it was built here to avoid toll charges in Bakewell market place. Just upstream of Holme Bridge is the site of Lumford Mill, originally built by Richard Arkwright in 1778 as a cotton mill, who altered the course of the river to create a large mill pond to power his waterwheel. At its height the mill employed around 350 people, mainly women and children, although the original mill burnt down in 1868 and was rebuilt. A row of millworkers' cottages and mill pond remain.

The Monsal Trail is an eight-and-a-half mile walking route between Bakewell and Chee Dale along the track-bed of the former Midland Railway route from London to Manchester. From Derby, the railway followed the Derwent Valley as far as Rowsley before heading west up through the limestone valleys of the River Wye to Buxton. The railway reached Rowsley in 1849, Buxton in 1863 and finally Manchester in 1867. Its construction was extremely controversial, particularly the section through Monsal Dale and Miller's Dale, which caused a national outcry with John Ruskin lamenting *"...you blasted its rocks away, heaped thousands of tons of shale into its lovely stream. The valley is gone and the Gods with it, and now every fool in Buxton can be at Bakewell in half an hour and every fool in Bakewell at Buxton; which you think a lucrative process of exchange –*

*you fools everywhere."* The line closed in 1968 above Rowsley and was disused for 12 years before the Peak District National Park created the Monsal Trail walking route. Time is a great healer and the embankments and viaducts have become a much loved part of the landscape as well as a haven for wildlife. Of particular note is Great Longstone Station as well as the incredible view from Monsal Head with the famous viaduct dominating, its huge arches rising 80-ft above the river. *Addendum: The four blocked-up railway tunnels along the Monsal Trail, including Headstone Tunnel at Monsal Head, will re-open during 2011 as part of a new cycle trail between Buxton and Bakewell.*

Ashford in the Water is perhaps the prettiest village in the Peak District with its ancient bridge, lovely church, cricket pitch, good pubs and well-stocked shop. It is famed for its attractive yet rather squat 17th Century packhorse bridge known as Sheepwash Bridge that stands above the original ford that gave the village its name. Beside the bridge are old pens from where sheep were dipped in the river to give their fleeces a 'spring clean' before clipping. This river crossing has been in use since at least the Iron Age for it lies on the Portway, a prehistoric trackway that stretched north to south through the heart of the Peak District connecting settlements and religious sites. Holy Trinity Church was greatly restored in the 1870's, although parts of the tower date from the 13th Century. Inside are memorials made from Ashford Black Marble, a highly polished local limestone that was popular in Victorian times. There are also four Maiden's Crowns, rare survivors of an ancient custom. These funeral garlands date back to the 18th Century and are made from paper rosettes attached to a wooden frame that would have been carried at the funeral of young unmarried women. Ashford is also famed for its well dressings that take place every year in early June. This custom dates back to pagan times when people worshipped a constant and pure supply of water, especially in the White Peak where the pervious limestone bedrock means that streams are few and far between. As Christianity replaced pagan worship, many of the ancient traditions were simply given new Christian meaning. Over the centuries, well dressings have progressed from simple offerings to lavish floral displays where flower petals and other natural materials are mounted on boards of clay to create vivid pictorial scenes, predominantly Biblical. Over thirty villages throughout the Peak District have well dressings during the summer.

# BAKEWELL SUNDAY WALK

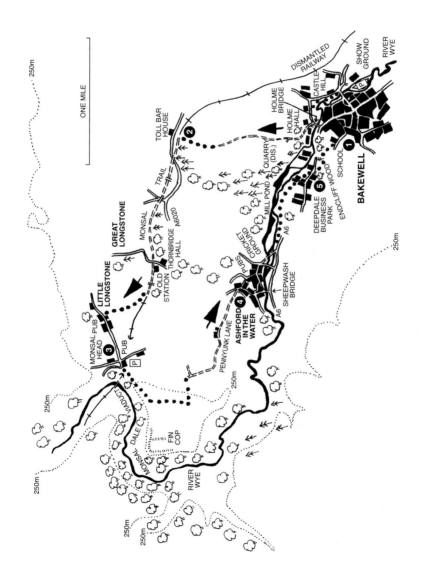

25

# THE WALK

1. From the roundabout in the centre of Bakewell (with your back to the Rutland Arms), walk through the town centre down along Bridge Street to reach the ancient bridge across the Wye, immediately after which take the FP to the left (SP 'Scot's Garden'). Follow the riverside path to reach two small wooden gates beside a meander along the river, after which join a clear path beside some steps. Follow this path to the left alongside the river at first then straight on across the meadow to reach a small wall-gate that leads onto a lane. Turn left along the lane to reach a junction of lanes and tracks beside Holme Bridge (Packhorse Bridge) at the entrance to Riverside Business Park. Turn right (SP) up along the track (away from Holme Bridge) passing between the houses then, after a short distance where the track forks just beyond the row of Lumford Cottages, follow the middle track bearing slightly to the left uphill. Follow this rough, stony track rising up through woodland to reach a gate at the top of the woods. Head through the gate and follow the track up across a field then, where this stony track swings round to the left towards a gate and old quarry workings, head straight on (markerpost) along a grassy track up to reach a wall-stile beside a gate at the top of the field at the start of a walled track. Follow this walled grassy track straight on for 0.75 miles, gently rising up over the broad ridge then steadily down to reach the Monsal Trail across your path (railway track-bed).

2. Turn left along the track-bed and follow this straight on for just over a mile passing over and beneath several bridges to reach the former Great Longstone Station. Carry straight on along the old railway line passing the former station and continue along the Monsal Trail passing beneath a railway bridge, about 200 yards after which the stony track forks - take the FP to the right over a wall-stile (SP 'Little Longstone, Monsal Head'). Turn left after the stile down alongside the wall to reach a small gate in the bottom corner of the field, after which head straight on across fields to join the road at Little Longstone. Turn left along the road and follow this up through the

village passing the Packhorse Inn, then carry on leaving the village behind to reach a T-junction opposite the Monsal Head Hotel.

3. Take the turning opposite to the right towards 'Upper Dale, Cressbrook' passing in front of the Monsal Head Hotel *(viewpoint across Monsal Dale to your right)* then, as you reach the brow of the hill where the road bends sharply down to the right, take the FP to the left off this bend (SP 'Ashford, Monsal Dale'). Follow this path straight on for a few paces then, where the path forks, follow the left-hand path (SP 'Ashford') gradually slanting up across the steep hillside, through a bridlegate then up some steps to join a wall on your left along the top of the steep wooded bank. Follow the path straight on across the top of the wooded bank alongside the wall on your left *(views through trees across Monsal Dale)* very gently rising up for just over 0.25 miles to reach a gate tucked away in the wall corner just beyond two benches (SP 'Ashford'). Head through the gate and follow the walled path straight on, passing through two gates (the wall on your right temporarily disappears between these two gates) then continue straight on along the walled path to reach a third gate at the end of the walled path. Head through the gate and carry straight on alongside the wall on your left to reach a small wall-gate to your left in the bottom field corner. Head through this wall-gate and walk down across the field keeping close to the wall on your right to reach a squeeze-stile beside a gate in the bottom right corner of the field at the top of a walled track (Pennyunk Lane). Follow this track straight on (ignore track to the left after a short distance) gradually winding down for one mile to reach the road opposite Highfield Farm at the top end of Ashford in the Water.

4. Turn right and follow the road down into Ashford, heading straight on towards 'Bakewell, Matlock' at the road junction beside the small circular 'green'. Continue along this road bending round to the left *(Sheepwash Bridge to your right off this bend)* passing Holy Trinity Church then curving to the right around the Ashford Arms to reach a T-junction with the A6020 opposite the cricket pitch. At the road, take the lane opposite to the right and follow this straight on (cricket pitch on your left) over the old road-bridge across the Wye to reach

the main road (A6). At the road, turn left along the roadside path for 25 yards then take the FP to the left through a small wall-gate (SP). After the wall-gate, follow the path to the right across undulating pastures (waymarkers) heading downstream with the wooded banks of the Wye just across to your left to reach a small gate in a fence (weirs draining Ashford Lake across to your left). Head through two small gates then over a stile, after which follow the path bearing slightly to the right away from the river to reach an enclosed path that leads between houses to join a street on the outskirts of Bakewell. At the road, follow the enclosed path opposite just to the right that quickly leads to a stile, after which follow the clear path ahead across the field (leaving the houses behind) bearing gradually round to the right to reach the main road (A6) opposite Deepdale Business Park.

5. Turn left down along the road for about 100 yards then, where the road curves to the left, take the FP to the right (immediately after the business park) that leads up into Endcliff Wood (SP). Follow the path climbing steeply up through the woods - the path soon levels out and leads on through the woods to emerge out onto a sports field beside a wooden hut (St Anselm's School). Head to the right along the sports field boundary passing to the right of a large sports hall building and across the parking area to join a road. Turn left down along this road then, where the road forks at the bottom of Stanedge Road, bear to the right down passing All Saints Church back into the centre of Bakewell.

# BASLOW

*The bustling village of Baslow stands watch over the northern entrance to Chatsworth where a number of important routes converge to cross the River Derwent. Baslow is made up several 'separate' settlements including West End, Bridge End, Over End, Nether End and Far End, each with their own distinctive character. The oldest part is Bridge End where there has been a ford across the Derwent since the earliest times, later replaced by a wooden bridge that was replaced in 1603 by the present three-arched Old Bridge. Beside this bridge is the tiny Watchman's Hut where the village men would guard this important river crossing and where tolls were also collected. Thankfully, this Old Bridge has now been bypassed by the more modern Devonshire Bridge just downstream. Close by is St Anne's Church, with its squat spire, battlemented parapets and unusual clock face with 'VICTORIA 1897' rather than numerals. This site has been used as a place of worship since pre-Conquest days, however, the present church dates from around 1300 when the spire and nave were built, although alterations were made in the 19th Century by the Duke of Devonshire. Nether End clusters around the northern entrance to Chatsworth Park, a village in itself with shops and inns overlooking Goose Green. The path into Chatsworth Park crosses an old bridge across Bar Brook beyond which is a row of thatched cottages, a rarity in Derbyshire. This part of Baslow is closely linked to the Chatsworth Estate, although up until the 19th Century much of Baslow, in particular Nether End, formed part of the Duke of Rutland's estate, who still own nearby Haddon Hall. Over the years they have sold off land and buildings to the Chatsworth Estate as well as local people.*

## THE VILLAGE

Baslow boasts four pubs, two plush hotels, a café, bistro, Italian restaurant, general stores, newsagent, gift and craft shops, public toilets, large car park and a regular bus service.

## ACCOMMODATION

Tourist Information Centre, Bakewell:     01629 816558

## BASLOW PUBS

**Devonshire Arms, Baslow:**     **01246 582551**
This large, comfortable pub overlooks Goose Green in the heart of Nether End. Inside, there are plenty of cosy corners and comfy sofas as well as a food carvery and games area.

**Rowley's Restaurant and Bar, Baslow:**     **01246 583880**
Formerly the Prince of Wales, this traditional pub underwent a complete transformation during 2006 and is now a contemporary bar/restaurant with an emphasis on good food. No accommodation.

**Rutland Arms, Baslow:**     **01246 582276**
Situated next to the Old Bridge across the River Derwent, this traditional pub boasts a wonderful riverside beer garden. Inside, a central bar serves the separate lounge and games areas, which are warmed by open fires.

**Wheatsheaf Hotel, Baslow:**     **01246 582240**
This attractive three-storey Georgian coaching inn boasts a warm and welcoming interior with a large lounge/bar and restaurant that serves food all day. Outside, there is a delightful patio and beer garden with children's play area.

## PUBS ALONG THE WALKS

| | |
|---|---|
| Devonshire Arms, Pilsley: | 01246 583258 |
| Eyre Arms, Hassop: | 01629 640390 |
| Derwentwater Arms, Calver: | 01433 639211 |
| Bridge Inn, Calver Bridge: | 01433 630415 |
| Chequers Inn, Froggatt: | 01433 630231 |

# Baslow Walking Weekend
# - Saturday Walk -
*Baslow, Chatsworth House, Edensor, Pilsley,*
*Hassop & Bank Wood*

## WALK INFORMATION

| | |
|---|---|
| Highlights | Chatsworth Park and Capability Brown, the Palace of the Peak, a hotchpotch of buildings, quiet lanes and ancient track-ways, some fine Peakland pubs and wonderful woodland walks. |
| Distance | 10.5 miles          Time          4 - 5 hours |
| Maps | OS Explorer OL24 |
| Refreshments | Pubs at Baslow, Pilsley, Hassop and Calver. Shops and/or cafés at Baslow, Chatsworth House, Edensor, Pilsley and Calver. |
| Terrain | Clear field paths, stony tracks and quiet country lanes lead from Baslow, through Chatsworth Park to reach Pilsley. A rough track then leads quite steeply down to reach the A619 from where a clear track heads through woodland to reach Hassop. After a short stretch of road-walking, a path heads along the top of a wooded bank virtually all the way to Calver, from where a riverside path leads back to Baslow. |
| Ascents | Handley Lane - 247 metres above sea level |
| Caution | This walk involves some stretches along country lanes - face oncoming traffic. Take extra care crossing the B6012 at Edensor, the A619 to the north-west of Pilsley and the B6001 through Hassop. The descent from the top of wooded bank above Bramley Wood is steep. |

Chatsworth Park extends for 1,000 acres around Chatsworth House, one of England's finest stately homes known as the 'Palace of the Peak', home of the Cavendish family for over 400 years. Chatsworth Park originally formed the western edge of Sherwood Forest and still has ancient oaks as well as roaming deer, cattle and sheep. In 1549, Bess of Hardwick and her second husband Sir William Cavendish, a wealthy aristocrat, bought the manor of Chatsworth and built a mansion house; their son William became the 1st Earl of Devonshire in 1618. The present Palladian-style house was built between 1686 and 1707 by the 4th Earl (who became the 1st Duke in 1694 for his part in bringing William of Orange to the throne) on the site of the Tudor mansion house. The layout of Chatsworth Park and the formal gardens surrounding the house are largely the creation of the 4th Duke during the mid 18th Century, who employed 'Capability' Brown to landscape the park whilst the stable block (1763) and Chatsworth Bridge (1762) were built by James Paine, a famous architect. Favourable marriages coupled with revenues from their extensive lands and mining interests during the late 18th and early 19th centuries meant that the Cavendish family became extremely wealthy. During the 19th Century the 6th Duke employed Joseph Paxton as head gardener who improved the formal gardens with the addition of the Emperor Fountain with its 280ft gravity-fed plume of water as well as the now-demolished Great Conservatory - the forerunner of the Crystal Palace which Paxton designed for the Great Exhibition of 1851. Inside, Chatsworth House boasts a wealth of treasures including one of Europe's finest private art collections as well as superbly painted rooms and halls. It is still the family home of the Duke and Duchess of Devonshire.

Queen Mary's Bower stands near Chatsworth Bridge, a rare survivor of Bess of Hardwick's original building that is named after Mary Queen of Scots, who was held captive at Chatsworth during the 16th Century. Another relic of Tudor Chatsworth is the Hunting Tower that rises above the wooded escarpment, where ladies could follow the progress of a hunt below. The Chatsworth Estate stretches far beyond Chatsworth

Park and includes estate villages, grouse moors and working farms. Of all the estate villages, Edensor (pronounced 'Ensor') is the finest with the spire of St Peter's Church pointing towards the heavens surrounded by a cluster of houses each with their own architectural style. The original village stood nearer the river but was pulled down by the 4th Duke as it spoilt the view from his house! It was not until 1838 that the 6th Duke began to rebuild a new village in a different location. The focal point is St Peter's Church, built in 1869 on the site of the original 14th Century church by renowned architect Sir George Gilbert Scott. The church has many interesting features including the monument to Bess of Hardwick's two sons, whilst in the churchyard are several Cavendish graves. Kathleen Kennedy lies buried beside the Dukes, widow of William Cavendish, the Marquess of Hartington, and daughter of Joseph Kennedy, Ambassador of the United States to Great Britain. She died in a plane crash in 1948 aged just 28, four years after her husband had been killed in the Second World War. Her brother, John F. Kennedy, visited her grave a few months before his assassination.

Close by is the delightful estate village of Pilsley, a cluster of 18th and 19th Century houses with the blue livery of the Chatsworth Estate. Situated on a shelf of land high above the Derwent Valley, the village was first mentioned in the Domesday Book. When the 4th Duke razed Edensor village, many inhabitants were re-housed at Pilsley. Centuries ago, this was a busy place where several important packhorse routes converged; indeed, in 1835 the village had three alehouses and two inns. The village of Hassop dates back many centuries, an attractive mixture of farms and cottages centred on a road junction beside the gates to Hassop Hall, where you will find the impressive Catholic Church, built in 1818 as the Eyre family chapel. The Eyre family bought the manor of Hassop in 1498, an influential local family who held a score of manors throughout the Derwent, Hope and Ashop valleys. They were staunch Roman Catholics during a period of religious persecution. The present hall dates from the 17th Century, with 19th Century additions, and was their home until 1853 when it passed out of their ownership following a series of contested wills. It is now a privately-owned hotel.

# BASLOW SATURDAY WALK

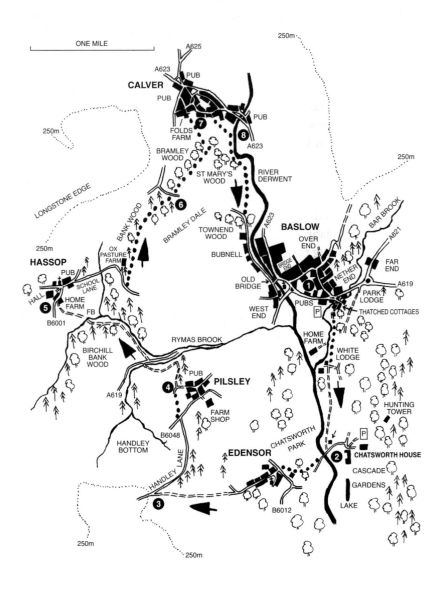

34

# THE WALK

1. From Goose Green in the Nether End area of Baslow (with your back to the car park) turn right along the road then, where it bends round to the left at the end of the village green (café on corner), take the turning straight on ('Dead End' sign) over a bridge across Bar Brook. After the bridge, turn immediately right along a lane (SP 'Chatsworth') passing in front of some thatched cottages and through a metal squeeze-stile beside a gate, after which follow the wide gravel path straight on then skirting to the left around Plantation Cottage to reach the Cannon kissing-gate (revolving metal gate) on the edge of Chatsworth Park. Head through the gate and follow the wide path straight on (SP 'Chatsworth House, Queen Mary's Bower') to soon join a metalled lane, which you follow straight on to reach a crossroads of lanes/tracks beside White Lodge gatehouse. Continue straight on along the gravel track heading across Chatsworth Park for a further 0.75 miles to reach the road beside Chatsworth Bridge just beyond Queen Mary's Bower *(Chatsworth House across to your left)*.

2. Turn right over Chatsworth Bridge across the River Derwent, immediately after which follow the gravel path branching off to the right gradually bearing away from the road. Follow this path gently rising up across Chatsworth Park, through an area of scattered trees then down to reach the B6012 opposite Edensor village. Cross the road and head through the white gates into Edensor then, where the road forks after a short distance, follow the right-hand lane passing to the right of the church. Continue along this lane rising up through the village then, at the last of the houses at the top of the village, carry straight on along the lane ('Unsuitable for Motors' sign) out of Edensor. After a further 250 yards the lane forks - head straight on along the left-hand stony track (ignore lane bending round to right) and follow this climbing steadily up for 0.75 miles to reach a road (Handley Lane).

3. Turn right along Handley Lane and follow this gently dropping down, with fine views down into Handley Bottom to your left, for

0.75 miles to reach the B6048. Cross over the road and take the FP opposite over a stile (SP), after which bear slightly to the right across the field to reach a wall-stile on the other side that leads onto the top of an enclosed grassy track. Follow this track straight on then curving round to the right (views down into the valley of Rymas Brook) to join a clear, gravel track on a sharp bend just on the outskirts of Pilsley. *(Our route turns left here, however, a short detour to the right takes you into the centre of Pilsley and the Devonshire Arms).*

4. Turn left along the clear track (SP) and follow it heading downhill, then bending to the left heading more steeply down to reach the A619. Turn right along the road (take care) for 50 yards then take the stony track to the left through a gate ('Unsuitable for Motors'). Follow this track straight on to soon reach a gate across the track, after which continue straight on along the track with woodland on your right at first then on through Birchill Bank Wood (keep to the clear track all the way) and down to reach a ford/FB across Rymas Brook after 0.75 miles. After the stream, continue up along the stony track for a further 0.25 miles, passing through the edge of a farmyard to join the B6001 at Hassop.

5. Turn right along the road *(take care and use the pavement)* and follow this through Hassop, bearing round to the right towards 'Calver' at the road junction near the gates to Hassop Hall and on passing the Eyre Arms just after which (on the edge of the village) take the turning to the right (sign 'Baslow'). Follow this road (School Lane) straight on gently dropping down into a shallow valley then rising up and bending up to the right passing the entrance to Ox Pasture Farm. Continue along the road gently rising up and bending round to the left (road levels out) then, just after the woodland ends on your left, take the FP to the left over a wall-stile just after a gate (SP). After the stile, bear left across the field alongside the field boundary/ woodland on your left up to reach a stile in the top left corner. Cross the stile and follow the clear path straight on along the top of a steep wooded bank (with a wall on your right), with the occasional clearing offering views towards Longstone Edge. The path leads through Bank Wood South and then Bank Wood North, at the end

of which the path heads through a wall-gate to your right then continues straight on down to quickly reach a lane.

6. At the lane, take the FP opposite to the left (SP) and follow the clear path straight on along the edge of Bramley Wood heading along the top of the wooded ridge (with woodland to your left and a wall on your right) for almost 0.5 miles then, as you approach the end of the ridge, a wonderful bird's eye view of Calver unfolds before you. Continue straight on along the path gently dropping down then, where the wall on your right bends away, carry straight on down through woodland to quickly reach a junction of paths. Head left for a few paces then follow the clear path bending sharply down to the left slanting down across the wooded hillside then, where this path forks after a short distance (waymarker), follow the clearer path bending to the right steeply down across the sparsely wooded hillside to reach a stile tucked away in the fence corner at the bottom of the wooded bank. Cross the stile and follow the path straight on across the field down into a shallow valley then rising up to join a wall on your right which you follow straight on to reach a stile that leads onto an enclosed path on the edge of Calver. Follow this path straight on (ignore path off to the right) that soon joins a gravel driveway which you follow to the left then right through the former farmyard of Folds Farm to reach the High Street through Calver.

7. Turn right down along the High Street to reach the triangular road junction in the heart of the village with an old lamp standard *(short detour up along Lowside just before this junction to reach the Derwentwater Arms)*. At this junction, follow the road round to the right (Main Street) heading down through the village passing Calver Methodist Church, a short distance after which take the enclosed path to the right immediately after the entrance to the Village Hall (just after the small parking area and short section of culverted stream). Follow this path straight on between the houses to reach a stile on the edge of Calver, after which head straight on across the field keeping close to the hedge/houses on your left to reach a wall-stile beside a gate, then follow the path straight on across fields to join the clear riverside path along the banks of the River Derwent.

8. Turn right and follow the riverside path to soon reach a squeeze-stile that leads into St Mary's Wood, after which follow the broad path curving round to the left (following a curve in the river) then, after a short distance, follow the path as it bears to the right away from the river. Follow this path straight on heading along the foot of a wooded bank to soon emerge from the woods, where you carry straight on along the broad path (still heading along the foot of the sparsely wooded bank) to reach a gate, after which continue straight on then follow the path as it bears very slightly to the right to quickly reach a squeeze-stile. Head through the squeeze-stile and follow the path across the field to reach a gate that leads onto a road. Turn left along the road and follow this up through woodland then gently down through the hamlet of Bubnell to reach the Old Bridge across the River Derwent that leads into Baslow (Bridge End). Turn right along the main road back to reach Goose Green (Nether End).

# Baslow Walking Weekend
# - Sunday Walk -
## *Baslow, River Derwent, Froggatt Edge*
## *& Wellington's Monument*

## WALK INFORMATION

Highlights    Walking along the Derwent, Colditz Castle, the finest edge walk in the Peak District, a stone with something to prove and Wellington's Monument.

Distance    6.5 miles       Time       3 hours

Maps    OS Explorer OL24

Refreshments    Pubs and cafés at Baslow and Calver Bridge. Pub at Froggatt.

Terrain    Clear riverside path from Baslow to Froggatt from where there is quite a steep climb up along a rough path through woodland onto Froggatt Edge. A clear, wide path then heads south along the top of Froggatt Edge, Curbar Edge and Baslow Edge, with magnificent views across the Derwent Valley. The path leads past the Eagle Stone to join Bar Road near Wellington's Monument (stony track) which leads back down into Baslow.

Ascents    Curbar Edge - 335 metres above sea level

Caution    The climb up onto Froggatt Edge is quite steep along a rough stony path. Take care crossing the A625 at Froggatt. Keep well away from the edge of Froggatt Edge and Curbar Edge - sheer drops and hidden crevices.

# POINTS OF INTEREST

Calver Bridge spans the River Derwent, a fine 18th Century structure that links Calver with its neighbour Curbar, now by-passed by a modern bridge. This has been an important river crossing for centuries, beyond which the old turnpike road to Chesterfield climbed up through the 'nick' in the skyline known as Curbar Gap. Just upstream is Calver Mill, originally built in 1778 but rebuilt in 1804 by Richard Arkwright following a fire. This watermill originally spun cotton and once employed around 200 people, although it later made stainless steel sinks and is now apartments. It was used as Colditz Castle in the 1970's TV series Colditz.

A delightful sylvan riverside path leads from New Bridge to Froggatt Bridge from where a steep path climbs through ancient woodland to emerge at the base of Froggatt Edge, a popular spot for climbers. Froggatt Edge and Curbar Edge are perhaps the most popular of the eastern gritstone edges as the path along the top offers a wonderful high level route with incredible views across the Derwent Valley. 350 million years ago, a warm tropical sea covered what is now the Peak District. Over millions of years, countless tiny sea creatures fell to the bottom of this sea and were compressed to form a thick layer of limestone. Then, around 300 million years ago, great rivers flowed over this newly-formed limestone depositing sand and mud which, over time, were compressed to form sedimentary rocks known as gritstones. These rock layers were later pushed up by movements in the earth's plates to form a huge dome, dissected by river valleys. Over aeons, the gritstone dome has weathered away so much so that it has completely disappeared in the central and southern areas of the Peak District exposing the limestone beneath, which has created the White Peak landscape. To the north, east and west the dome has remained and now forms the heather moors of the Dark Peak. In the east, the boundary of this weathered gritstone dome has created an escarpment of sheer edges that tower above the Derwent Valley.

The Eagle Stone stands near the southern end of Baslow Edge, a large tor of resistant gritstone. A local tradition was for the young men of Baslow to climb to the top to prove their prowess before they were deemed fit to marry! Just beyond is Wellington's Monument, built in 1866 by Mr Wrench, a Baslow doctor who had previously served as an army surgeon in Crimea and India.

*Baslow*

John A. Ivo?
2006

# BASLOW SUNDAY WALK

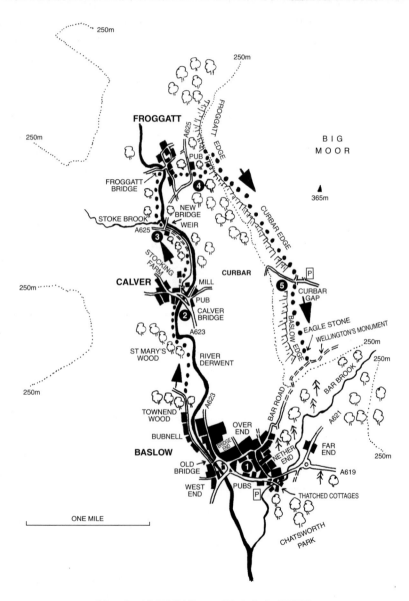

# THE WALK

1. From the Old Bridge across the River Derwent beside the Rutland Arms (Bridge End area of Baslow), cross the Old Bridge and turn immediately right. Follow this road gently rising up through the hamlet of Bubnell then, after the last of the houses, continue straight on along the road down through Townend Wood. The road soon emerges from the woods and bends round to the left at which point take the FP to the right through a bridlegate beside a gate (SP). After the gate, bear slightly left across the middle of the field along a grassy path (ignore clearer tracks to the right) to reach a squeeze-stile in a section of wall, after which follow the path bearing to the right to join a wall on your right which you follow straight on along a broad path to soon reach a gate across your path. Head through the gate and follow the broad path straight on along the foot of a wooded bank that leads into St Mary's Wood. Continue straight on along the broad path to join the banks of the River Derwent and on to reach a squeeze-stile at the end of the woods. Follow the clear riverside path straight on then, as you reach the houses of Calver, cross a FB over a side-stream then carry straight on along the riverside path (houses on your left), passing beneath the modern road bridge and up to join the road beside Calver Bridge across the Derwent (boundary between Calver and Curbar).

2. Turn left along the road then almost immediately right along a metalled lane towards Calver Mill (SP 'New Bridge, Froggatt'). Follow this lane straight on then, where it forks at the entrance to Calver Mill, carry straight on towards Stocking Farm. As you reach the farm buildings, pass to the right of the ornate stone-built barn and through a kissing-gate beside a field gate (waymarker). After the kissing-gate, head straight on across the field to join a clear path in the far right corner beside the tree-shaded mill race (marker-post). Follow this clear path straight on into woodland (with the mill race on your right and the River Derwent just beyond) to soon reach a stile beside a gate. Cross the stile and follow the broad path through

43

woodland alongside the old mill race to join a track beside an open-sided barn at the end of the woods, which you follow straight on passing some cottages to join the A625 beside New Bridge across the River Derwent.

3. At the road take the FP directly opposite (SP) and follow the riverside path through woodland (with the Derwent on your right) through Calver Marshes nature reserve and over a small FB across Stoke Brook, after which the path quickly re-joins the riverbank. Follow this riverside path straight on heading upstream along the wooded banks of the Derwent for 0.5 miles to reach the road at Froggatt Bridge. Turn right over the bridge, after which turn right and follow this road heading through Froggatt (with the Derwent on your right) then, just before the road bends to the right, take the FP to the left through a squeeze-stile beside a gate just after the entrance to Meadow Croft (SP). Follow the clear path straight on climbing up across the sparsely wooded hillside (with Froggatt Edge rising above) to reach the A625 near the Chequers Inn *(take care - fast road)*.

4. Cross the road and take the FP opposite into woodland (SP). Follow the clear, rough path gradually snaking up through woodland to reach a bridlegate set in a wall. Head through the bridlegate and continue up along the rocky path climbing steadily up across the wooded hillside to emerge at the base of the gritstone outcrops of Froggatt Edge. Follow the path to the right below these outcrops gradually rising up through a break in the outcrops to reach a wide path along the top of Froggatt Edge. Turn right and follow this clear path for 1.25 miles gently rising up across Curbar Edge (keep to the clear, wide path all the way) to eventually reach a kissing-gate beside a white gate at the southern end of Curbar Edge just above the parking area at Curbar Gap (hidden by trees). Head through this gate, just after which the path forks - follow the right-hand track winding down to reach the road at Curbar Gap.

5. At the road take the stony track opposite up through a bridlegate beside a metal gate (SP), after which head straight on along the broad path alongside the wall on your left, with Baslow Edge just

across to your right. After a short distance, follow the broad path gently curving round to the left alongside the wall on your left (ignore the path branching off to the right) gradually bearing away from Baslow Edge then, where this wall turns sharp left, carry straight on along the track across open moorland for a further 0.5 miles to reach the Eagle Stone (large outcrop). Continue straight on along the broad path passing to the right of the Eagle Stone to soon join a clear track (Bar Road) across your path along the top of a wooded escarpment. *(Short detour to the left to reach Wellington's Monument)*. Turn right along this track and follow it slanting down across the hillside to reach a gate at the top of a metalled lane. Head through the gate and follow the lane straight on gently dropping down then, where the lane forks, follow the lane bending sharply down to the right (ignore the track to the left towards the barns) and follow this down into Baslow. As you reach the road junction and small triangular green at Over End, either turn right along School Lane back to reach Bridge End or left along Eaton Hill down to reach Nether End.

# CASTLETON

*Castleton is an attractive village of grey-stone houses sheltered beneath a great arc of hills at the head of the Hope Valley with Mam Tor dominating. Situated at the point where the White Peak limestone meets the Dark Peak gritstone, the surrounding landscape offers an unrivalled diversity of terrain. The limestone hills to the west and south were formed 350 million years ago as a coral reef in a warm tropical sea. Since Roman times, these hills have been mined for lead and the semi-precious Blue John stone, a unique type of fluorspar. Levels were driven into the hillsides and natural limestone caves opened up, four of which can be visited today as show caves including Peak Cavern, Speedwell Cavern, Treak Cliff Cavern and Blue John Cavern. Castleton developed as a planned settlement in the protective shadow of Peveril Castle, which stands proudly on a dramatic promontory high above the town. It was built in 1086 by William Peverel, trusted knight of William the Conqueror, although some say he was his illegitimate son! The castle was used to manage the lucrative local lead mines as well as the surrounding Royal Forest of the Peak, a Norman hunting preserve.*
*In 1155 the castle and its estate were forfeited to the Crown after Peverel's son rebelled against Henry II, who subsequently strengthened its defences with the addition of the keep, hall and gatehouse from where a watchful eye could be kept on the rebellious barons. In 1372 the castle passed to John of Gaunt and became part of the Duchy of Lancaster estate, although by now it was obsolete as a defensive building and was only used to administer the mines and hunting grounds. By the late 15th Century the castle had all but been abandoned.*

## THE VILLAGE

Castleton is a thriving village where you will find six pubs, several B&B's, Youth Hostel, general stores and Post Office, outdoor pursuits shop, gift shops, craft shops, restaurant, cafés, fish & chip shop, Castleton Information Centre, bus service, large car park, garage, toilets, Peveril Castle and four Show Caves.

## ACCOMMODATION

Castleton Information Centre:          01433 620679

## CASTLETON PUBS

**The George, Castleton:**          **01433 620238**
This classic Peakland pub has bags of character. The cosy bar boasts a flagstone floor, large stone fireplace and plenty of intimate corners for a quiet drink. There is a separate dining room warmed by an open fire.

**Bull's Head, Castleton:**          **01433 620256**
Recently refurbished to a high standard, which has given this large pub more of a refined hotel feel rather than a village pub. Inside, the layout is open plan with separate drinking or dining areas including a rather cosy corner with leather armchairs around a large stone fireplace.

**The Castle, Castleton:**          **01433 620578**
Inside this historic 17th Century coaching inn there is a warren of rooms each with their own character. The pub oozes atmosphere with lots of cosy corners, low beams, stone-flagged floors, a superb inglenook fireplace and (reputedly) ghosts!

**Peaks Inn, Castleton:**          **01433 620247**
This warm and welcoming pub/restaurant is situated on the Hope road and is renowned for its good food, well-kept ales and lively atmosphere.

**Ye Olde Nag's Head, Castleton:**          **01433 620248**
This traditional 17th Century coaching inn boasts a comfortable bar with an original cast-iron Georgian hob-grate fireplace as well as a good selection of real ales.

**Ye Olde Cheshire Cheese:**          **01433 620330**
Walkers and their muddy boots are welcome, as the sign proclaims, in this traditional pub on the edge of Castleton. Inside you will find low beamed ceilings, lots of rooms and a stone fireplace as well as a noticeable lack of fruit machines or juke boxes - a quiet, civilised pub!

## PUBS ON THE WALKS

Woodroffe Arms, Hope:                                          01433 620351
Old Hall, Hope:                                                      01433 620160
Cheshire Cheese Inn, Hope:                                  01433 620381
Yorkshire Bridge Inn, Ladybower Reservoir: 01433 651361
Rambler Inn, Edale:                                               01433 670268
Old Nag's Head, Edale:                                          01433 670291

*Castleton*

# Castleton Walking Weekend
## - Saturday Walk -
### Castleton, Win Hill, Ladybower Reservoir & Hope Cross.

## WALK INFORMATION

| | |
|---|---|
| Highlights | The church of the foresters, ancient Saxon battles, Peakland's finest viewpoint, a vast reservoir, the ghosts of Roman soldiers and an old wayside cross. |
| Distance | 13.5 miles      Time      6 - 7 hours |
| Maps | OS Explorer OL1 |
| Refreshments | Pubs, shops and cafés at Castleton and Hope. Yorkshire Bridge Inn at Ladybower Reservoir. |
| Terrain | Field paths lead to Hope from where a track rises steadily up to Twitchill Farm high above the Hope Valley. A rough path then climbs steeply up onto moorland to reach Win Hill. There is a steady descent down along a muddy path to the Yorkshire Bridge and Ladybower Reservoir dam with fine views across the Derwent Valley. A level track skirts the shoreline of Ladybower Reservoir for 3 miles to reach the head of the reservoir from where a path climbs steeply through dense forest to reach Hope Cross. The Roman Road (stony track) is followed down across the hillside to join Edale Road from where field paths/tracks lead back to Castleton. |
| Ascents | Win Hill - 462 metres above sea level.<br>Hope Cross - 320 metres above sea level. |
| Caution | The climb up to Win Hill is steep and the summit exposed to the elements. The climb from the head of Ladybower Reservoir to Hope Cross is steep through dense forest. |

# POINTS OF INTEREST

There is more to Castleton that meets the eye, with its jumble of lanes, attractive buildings and hidden limestone gorges. From the centre of the village, Castle Street leads up past St Edmund's Church into the attractive Market Place with its small green. This solid church dates back to the 12th Century when it was known as the Church of the Peak Castle. Despite 19th Century restoration, much of interest remains including a Norman chancel arch and 17th Century box pews. A lane known as The Stones leads to the side of the 17th Century Castleton Hall, now a Youth Hostel, to reach Goosehill Bridge with its cluster of old cottages. The spectacular entrance to Peak Cavern is a short riverside walk away, the largest natural cave entrance in the British Isles that was believed to be the entrance to hell centuries ago, hence its alternative name of the Devil's Arse! Castleton is also famous for its Garland Day ceremony, which takes place on Oak Apple Day (29th May). The 'king', mounted on a horse and covered from head to knee by a garland of flowers, leads a procession around the streets of Castleton that finishes at the church where the garland is hoisted to the top of the tower. The ceremony commemorates the restoration of the monarchy, although the garland of flowers has pagan origins and represents the onset of spring.

Hope (Old English for 'valley') is a busy village situated beside the confluence of Peakshole Water and the River Noe where the Vale of Edale sweeps round to join the Hope Valley. This has always been a strategic spot with the remains of Navio Roman fort less than a mile away to the east. The prehistoric track-way known as the Portway also came through Hope, a north to south trading route through the heart of the Peak District that once connected important settlements and sites such as Mam Tor; many of these ancient routes later developed into packhorse trails and salt roads. By the time of the Domesday Book, Hope was already an important village within the Royal Forest of the Peak so much so that it gave its name to the valley. St Peter's Church dominates with its sturdy tower rising above the rooftops, once the main church within this Royal Forest with one of the largest parishes in England stretching as far as Buxton and Tideswell. The present church dates from the 13th and 14th Centuries and boasts two coffin stones of former Forest huntsmen as well as the shaft of a carved Saxon cross in the churchyard and grotesque gargoyles! Near the church stands the Woodroffe Arms, named after an influential local family who once held the position of the King's Foresters of the Peak.

The rocky outcrops of Win Hill rise up from a ridge of moorland that separates the Hope Valley from the Woodlands Valley. From its summit, a fine view unfolds across the Dark Peak with the hills of Mam Tor, Kinder Scout, Derwent Edge and Stanage Edge rising and falling into the distance, whilst far below Ladybower Reservoir floods the Woodlands and Upper Derwent valleys. According to legend, in the 7th Century the army of King Edwin of Northumbria camped here in preparation for a battle with the forces of King Cuicholm of Wessex who were encamped on Lose Hill across the valley. The battle ensued and King Edwin was victorious, hence the two names of 'win' and 'lose' hills. A more mundane explanation is that Win Hill is derived from the Saxon word for willow hill.

A scenically splendid descent leads down to Ladybower Reservoir. Built between 1935 and 1943, its earthen dam wall holds back 6,310 million gallons of water that supplies drinking water to Sheffield, Leicester, Derby and Nottingham. A track skirts the banks of this reservoir to reach a bridge across the River Ashop just above the head of the reservoir, from where a steep ascent ensues through forest up to Hope Cross on the old Roman Road between the forts at Glossop and the Hope Valley. This old stone guidepost dates from 1737 and once marked an important crossroads of packhorse routes across the hills between Hope, Glossop, Edale and Sheffield. Our walk follows the route of this Roman Road down across the hillside towards Hope, with superb views across the Vale of Edale, although make sure you get down before dusk as the ghosts of Roman soldiers are said to march along this ancient road!

# CASTLETON SATURDAY WALK

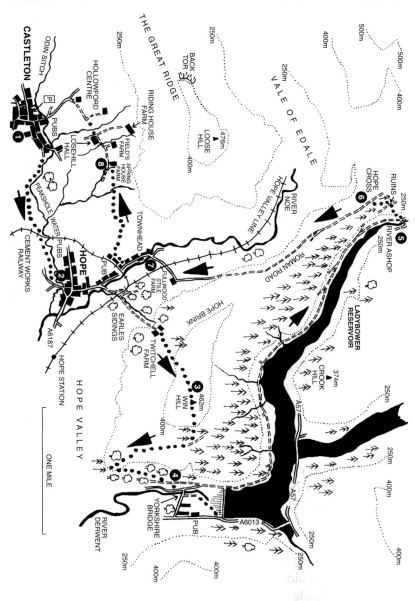

# THE WALK

1. From the centre of Castleton, follow the main road towards Hope, bending sharp left at Ye Olde Nag's Head then sharp right heading out of the village. Just before the road bends round to the left out of Castleton, take the walled track to the right (SP 'Hope'). Follow this track out of the village to join the banks of Peakshole Water beside a barn where you continue along the riverside track to soon reach a stile beside a gate at the end of the track. Cross the stile and walk straight on across the field alongside the fence/river on your left, curving round to the left to reach a tumbledown wall at the end of the field (cement works ahead), after which continue straight on alongside the fence on your right, leaving Peakshole Water to bend away to the left, to reach a stile in the top right corner of the field. Cross the stile and head straight on across three fields through a succession of squeeze-stiles/gates, then pass to the left side of the small tree-covered mound (markerposts) heading across the field to join the field boundary on your left that leads to a stile and the cement works railway. Cross the railway line *(take care)* and follow the path bearing very slightly to the left ahead along the top of a small bank above Peakshole Water for 0.5 miles to join a road. Turn left down along the road, over a bridge across Peakshole Water then up to reach the main road through Hope beside the Woodroffe Arms.

2. Turn right along the road then almost immediately left along Edale Road and follow this for 0.25 miles heading out of Hope then, where the road bends left, take Bowden Lane down to the right towards Hope Cemetery ('Dead End' sign). Follow this lane over a bridge across the River Noe then straight up to reach a railway bridge beside Earles Sidings. Pass beneath the bridge, immediately after which turn right along the lane through woodland then left along a farm lane heading steeply up across fields to reach Twitchill Farm. Head straight up through the farmyard and through a gate immediately to the right-hand side of the farmhouse, after which head straight up the steep hillside to reach a gate in a fence (SP). After the gate,

continue straight up the steep grassy hillside (SP 'footpath only' - ignore BW across your path) climbing up to reach a stile over a wall at the top of the field. After the stile, follow the eroded path slanting steeply up across the hillside to reach a large stone cairn at the top of the steep bank, where you carry on climbing more steadily up *(Win Hill comes into view)* to reach another large cairn and a tumbledown wall across your path at the top of the climb. A clear path now heads to the right across heather moorland up onto the summit outcrops of Win Hill.

3. Follow the path across the summit outcrops then quite steeply down to a stile across a wall, after which follow the path down through woodland to soon reach an enclosed track across your path and a junction of paths. Turn right (SP 'Thornhill') along the grassy track out of the woodland and follow this path straight on alongside a wall on your right for just over 0.25 miles to reach a junction of paths near a small stream and water trough. Carry straight on along the grassy path branching to the left (SP 'Thornhill') slanting down across the hillside through gorse bushes then, where it emerges from the gorse, you come to a wall corner (SP 'Thornhill') where you turn left down to a gate. After the gate, follow the path straight on gradually dropping down the hillside alongside a wall on your right through undergrowth to reach a gate, after which carry straight on down to reach a boggy area and a junction of paths. Turn left (SP 'Yorkshire Bridge') and follow the path slanting down across the wooded hillside, across fields and back through woodland to reach a road. At the road take the FP opposite to the left (SP 'Yorkshire Bridge') and follow this down through woodland to quickly join another road where you turn left to reach the Yorkshire Bridge across the Derwent.

4. Cross the Yorkshire Bridge, immediately after which turn left through a bridlegate (SP 'Heatherdene') and follow the path up to join a track. Turn left along this track then, just before a gate across the track, follow the path to the right (SP) that leads up to reach the eastern end of Ladybower Reservoir dam beside the A6013. *(Detour right along the A6013 to Yorkshire Bridge Inn)*. Turn left across the dam

wall to join a lane on the other side, where you turn right (lane soon becomes a stony track) and follow it skirting along the shoreline of Ladybower Reservoir for 3 miles to eventually reach a bridge across the River Ashop just beyond the head of the reservoir.

5. As you approach this bridge, take the track branching up to the left then, after a few paces, turn left up along a FP (SP 'Roman Road'). Follow the narrow path steeply up through the trees then double back on yourself winding up to reach some moss-covered ruinous buildings set on a shelf of land. Head straight across this flat shelf of land to quickly join an enclosed rough track immediately beyond the ruinous buildings - follow this track to the right then almost immediately left up along a wide path heading up across the steep hillside through dense forest. The path climbs up then levels out and leads to a stile over a fence at the edge of the forest, after which walk straight on for a few paces to join the Roman Road (stony track). Turn left through a gate to reach Hope Cross.

6. Follow the clear sandy/stony track straight on across the ridge alongside the forest at first, then gradually bearing away down to a gate in a wall. Just after the gate the track forks, head along the right-hand track heading straight on gently dropping down across the hillside. After a while, the track levels out slightly and heads across the upper slopes of the hillside, with Edale down to your right, then drops steadily down to reach a gate across the track at the start of an enclosed lane. Follow this lane heading steadily down, bending sharp right at the entrance to Fullwood Stile Farm down over a railway bridge to reach Edale Road beside Townhead Bridge across the River Noe.

7. Cross Townhead Bridge and follow the road towards 'Castleton, Hope' heading past the cluster of houses at Townhead then, just after the pavement on the right side of the road ends, cross the wall-stile to the right (SP) - *Cheshire Cheese Inn short detour straight on just beyond the railway bridge.* Head up the field through a wall-stile in the corner, then straight on across the next field alongside the hedge on your left to reach a stile in the field corner that leads into a

farmyard. As you enter the farmyard, turn immediately right through a wall-gate onto an enclosed path (SP 'Lose Hill') and follow this straight on to reach a stile at the end of the enclosed path that leads onto a sunken track. Follow this sunken track straight on to soon reach a small gate across your path, after which head through the small gate ahead to your right then left alongside the hedge to reach a kissing-gate just above the field corner that leads out onto a field. Head straight across the field to a stile beside a gate on the other side, however, turn immediately left before this gate (waymarker 'Castleton') and head across the field, keeping close to the field boundary on your right, to reach a stile beside a gate in the field corner. After the gate, head over some walk-boards then carry straight on alongside the hedge on your left at first then alongside the fence on your left across the top of a small bank, over two stiles across your path (on their own!) and then a small FB to reach a small gate in the bottom corner of the field that leads down over a FB across a stream. After the FB, head straight on alongside the hedge on your right across two fields, after which the path switches to the other side of the hedge to reach a track beside Spring House Farm.

8. Turn left through the gate into the farmyard and follow the driveway straight on to quickly reach a junction of tracks at the entrance to the farmhouse (beside the cattle grid) - take the track to the right (SP 'Castleton') and follow this straight on to reach a T-junction with the farm track leading to Field's Farm. Turn left and follow this track passing Losehill Hall on your left then, where the track bends sharp left around the boundary wall of Losehill Hall and a lane leads off to the right towards Riding House Farm, head straight on through a squeeze-stile out onto a field. Head straight on alongside the wall on your right and down through a small gate over stepping stones across a stream, after which carry straight on across the field to join a track beside a cattle grid in the bottom field corner. Turn left along this track and follow it to reach a road beside the entrance to Hollowford Centre. Turn left along this road back into Castleton.

# Castleton Walking Weekend - Sunday Walk -

*Castleton, Losehill Pike, the Great Ridge, Mam Tor & Cave Dale*

## WALK INFORMATION

Highlights     Incredible views, the Great Ridge, prehistoric hillforts, the shivering mountain, a spectacular limestone valley and a Norman cliff-top castle.

Distance     7.5 miles     Time     3 - 4 hours

Maps     OS Explorer OL1

Refreshments     Pubs, shops and cafés at Castleton. No facilities en route - take plenty of provisions with you.

Terrain     From Castleton, field paths lead steadily up towards Lose Hill with a final steep climb onto the summit (Losehill Pike). A clear path then heads along the top of the undulating ridge (flagged in places) up to the summit of Mam Tor (exposed to the elements). A path leads steeply down from the summit, then field paths and farm tracks head southwards before a path heads down through Cave Dale (steep, rocky path in places) back into Castleton.

Ascents     Mam Tor - 517 metres above sea level.

Caution     This walk involves a number of steep ascents and descents climbing to and from the Great Ridge. Keep well away from the edge of Back Tor (sheer cliffs), and keep to the path across the top of Mam Tor (sheer cliffs on its south-eastern edge). The path down through Cave Dale is rough underfoot and muddy in places.

# POINTS OF INTEREST

The summit of Lose Hill, known as Losehill Pike, is one of the finest viewpoints in the Peak District, a conical peak on the eastern nab of the Great Ridge from where the hillside drops steeply down into the Vale of Edale. The summit viewfinder helps pinpoint the hills, although the sheer scale of the surrounding landscape makes fine detail like names irrelevant. The summit of Lose Hill is known locally as Ward's Piece in memory of GHB Ward, renowned Sheffield rambler and access campaigner who donated this summit to The National Trust. The walk along the crest of the ridge between Lose Hill and Mam Tor is superb with wonderful views across the Hope Valley to your left and the Vale of Edale to your right with Kinder Scout rising above, deeply fissured by numerous cloughs.

Mam Tor - the Mother Mountain - is ringed by a prehistoric hill-fort, built by the native Celtic tribes some 3,000 years ago. There was a sizeable settlement within these ramparts with at least seventy hut circles identified as well as burial mounds. Iron Age hill-forts were not solely built for defense but were a bold statement of status and power by the local chieftain. They often had religious significance and were also used as a social centre for meetings and trade. Mam Tor is also known as the 'shivering mountain' as the unstable layers of shales and gritstone have been slipping away over thousands of years causing huge landslides. A massive landslide many years ago caused the eastern face of the mountain to completely fall away whilst, more recently, the main A625 between Sheffield and Chapel-en-le-Frith was swept away in 1979 - and the hillside is still moving at around 9cm a year. The final part of this walk heads through Cave Dale, a spectacular limestone valley where the path drops down through a narrow cleft between the crags with Peveril Castle perched high above. There is some dispute as to how this valley was formed; a collapsed cave system, the action of glacial meltwaters or the remains of an underwater channel formed when this whole area was submerged beneath a tropical sea.

*For more information about the Castleton Show Caves,*
*see Walking Weekend 4*

# CASTLETON SUNDAY WALK

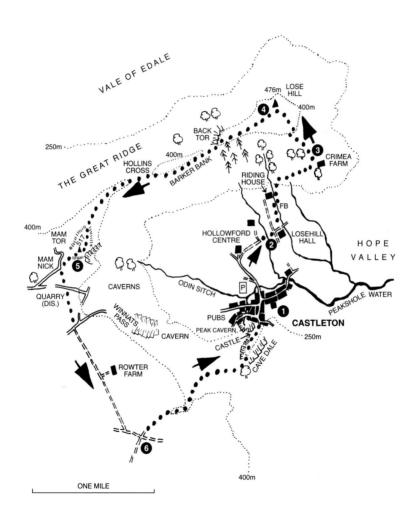

VALE OF EDALE

LOSE HILL
476m
400m
BACK TOR
250m
THE GREAT RIDGE
HOLLINS CROSS
400m
BARKER BANK
CRIMEA FARM
RIDING HOUSE
FB
400m
MAM TOR
517
HOLLOWFORD CENTRE
LOSEHILL HALL
HOPE VALLEY
MAM NICK
CAVERNS
ODIN SITCH
QUARRY (DIS.)
WINNAT'S PASS
PUBS
PEAK CAVERN
CASTLETON
250m
PEAKSHOLE WATER
CAVERN
CASTLE
CAVE DALE
ROWTER FARM
400m

ONE MILE

59

# THE WALK

1. From the centre of Castleton, follow the main road towards Hope, bending sharp left at Ye Olde Nag's Head then, where the road bends sharp right, turn left along Back Street and follow this lane down out of the village. Carry straight on for a further 0.5 miles to reach a fork in the road where you head to the right towards the Hollowford Centre for a short distance then, at the entrance to the Hollowford Centre, follow the walled track to your right (waymarker). Follow this track straight on then, where it bends sharp left over a cattle grid, turn right immediately after the cattle grid (SP) and follow the field-edge on your right to reach steeping stones across a stream and a small gate just beyond. Head through the gate and walk straight on alongside the field-edge on your left to reach a kissing-gate that leads onto a lane at a three-way junction.

2. Head straight on along the lane (SP 'Losehill') passing Losehill Hall on your right then, immediately after the Hall, take the FP to the left through a kissing-gate (SP 'Losehill'). Follow the path up across the field keeping close to the stream on your right, over a stile then carry on up across the next field. As you approach Riding House Farm, head to the right through a small gate down over a FB across the stream, after which follow the path up to the left then straight on across the field (stream to your left) to reach a stile beside a gate towards the top of the field (farm to your left) that leads over a small bridge across the stream and onto a farm track. Turn right up along the track then, just before the track turns right through a gate, take the FP to the right over a small FB/stile (SP). After the stile, head straight on alongside the fence on your left to join an enclosed rough track, which you follow straight on rising gently up to reach a stile beside a gate at the top of the enclosed track. After the gate, head straight on up across the field to reach two stiles (Crimea Farm ahead) and a crossroads of paths. After the stiles turn immediately left (SP 'Losehill') up to reach a small gate in the top field corner, after which follow the path bearing up to the right to quickly reach a wide grassy path across your path (above Crimea Farm).

*3.* Turn left up along this wide path (SP 'Losehill') and follow it climbing steadily up to soon join a wall on your right - carry on up alongside this wall then, as you near the top of the field *(with the summit of Lose Hill ahead)*, cross the stile to the right. After this stile, head up to the left over another stile (National Trust sign 'Losehill Pike & Ward's Piece') and follow the pitched-stone path steeply up to reach the summit of Losehill Pike.

*4.* At the summit, follow the flagged path to the left across the top of Lose Hill then down to reach a stile over a fence - carry straight on down into a 'dip' along the ridge (with Edale falling away to your right and the Hope Valley to your left) then gently rising up to reach a large cairn beside a solitary tree above a plantation on your left just before the cliff-edge of Back Tor *(warning - keep away from the edge)*. At this cairn, follow the fence on your left gently curving to the left then follow the path dropping steeply down to the side of Back Tor to reach a stile to your left at the bottom of the next 'dip'. Cross this stile then turn immediately right alongside the fence and follow the path across the top of the ridge gently rising up across Barker Bank then down to reach a 'crossroads' of paths at Hollins Cross (circular stone memorial). Carry straight on along the stone-flagged path across the top of the ridge and follow this curving gradually up to the left to reach the summit of Mam Tor.

*5.* Carry straight on across the top of Mam Tor along the stone-flagged path then drop steeply down steps to join a road at a sharp bend at Mam Nick. At the road turn immediately left down some steps (do not walk along the road) through a small gate (SP 'Cave Dale, Peak Forest') then head straight on along the grassy path down to reach the main road. Cross the road through the gate opposite to the left (SP) and follow the wide grassy path ahead for a short distance then, where it forks, follow the right-hand grassy track skirting around an old quarry then straight on to reach the road. At the road, head through the gate opposite to the right (SP) and follow the lane straight on to reach the entrance to Rowter Farm after 0.5 miles (lane becomes a track). Continue straight on along the stony track, through a gate and follow this for a further 0.5 miles to reach a T-junction with another track. Turn left along the walled track to quickly reach a crossroads of tracks after a gate.

6. Turn left at this crossroads (SP) through a gate along a short section of walled track and through another gate that leads out onto a field. Follow the grassy track bearing slightly to the right across the middle of the field (SP 'Castleton') then down into a grassy 'dip'. At the bottom of this dip, head right (blue waymarker) to quickly reach a wall-gate, after which follow the path straight on down to reach another wall-gate. Head through this wall-gate and follow the grassy/stony track straight on alongside a wall on your left gradually heading down into Cave Dale (valley sides become steeper) for 0.25 miles to reach a bridlegate across your path at the top of the ravine of Cave Dale *(Peveril Castle comes into view ahead)*. Head through the gate and follow the steep rocky path down through the narrow limestone valley passing outcrops and caves at first before the valley opens out slightly and the path becomes easier underfoot passing below Peveril Castle back down into Castleton.

*For an alternative walk from Castleton, please see Walking Weekend 4*

# EDALE
## *Grindsbrook Booth*

*Hemmed in by the towering escarpment of Kinder Scout to the north and the rounded hills of Mam Tor and the Great Ridge to the south, the Vale of Edale was once known as the 'island valley'. For centuries, it was virtually cut off from the outside world until the railway arrived in the late 19th Century. Along the valley floor are five clusters of farms known locally as booths although the largest of these, Grindsbrook Booth, is more commonly called Edale. The word 'booth' is derived from an old Scandinavian word for a shepherd's shelter. They all shelter below the towering escarpment of Kinder Scout that rises to just over 600 metres above sea level, an awe-inspiring landscape of wild moorland, jagged rocks and deep cloughs. This is where the Pennines really begin, and what a start they get off to! For such a small place Edale has a big reputation, known throughout the country for one thing - walking. Edale marks the official starting point of the Pennine Way, Britain's first National Trail. In 1935 Tom Stephenson, access campaigner and soon-to-be secretary of the Ramblers Association, wrote an article in the Daily Herald entitled 'Wanted: A Long Green Trail' where he championed the idea of a long trek across the backbone of Britain. At that time, much of the open country of the high Pennines was out of bounds for walkers, strictly the preserve of landowners and their gamekeepers, although the campaign to gain access to these forbidden hills was gathering pace. Thirty years later the Pennine Way officially opened, tracing a 268-mile route across the roof of the Pennines from Edale to Kirk Yetholm in the Scottish Borders.*

# THE VILLAGE

Edale is a popular walking centre and has plenty of facilities including two pubs, Youth Hostel (at Nether Booth), B&B's, campsites, cafés, shop, general stores, Post Office, large car park, train station, bus, toilets, phone box and the Moorland Visitor Centre.

# ACCOMMODATION

Moorland Visitor Centre, Edale:          01433 670207

# EDALE PUBS

**Rambler Inn, Edale:**          **01433 670268**
Surrounded by a large beer garden and children's play area, this popular hotel boasts several rooms warmed by open fires with stone or tiled floors and a good selection of Real Ale. Lots of photos of 'old Peakland' line the walls.

**Old Nag's Head, Edale:**          **01433 670291**
Dating back to 1577, this historic pub lies in the heart of Grindsbrook Booth and is the official starting point of the Pennine Way. The pub has plenty of character with a traditional bar area complete with open fire, several rooms, cosy corners and a quarry-tiled floor. Self-catering accommodation available.

# PUBS ON THE WALKS

The George, Castleton:                01433 620238
Bull's Head, Castleton:               01433 620256
The Castle, Castleton:                01433 620578
Peaks Inn, Castleton:                 01433 620247
Ye Olde Nag's Head, Castleton:        01433 620248
Ye Olde Cheshire Cheese:              01433 620330

# Edale Walking Weekend
## - Saturday Walk -
*Edale, Chapel Gate, Rushup Edge, Castleton*
*& Hollins Cross*

## WALK INFORMATION

Highlights     The old chapel road, a fine ridge walk with a surprise view, searching for Blue John, walk through the Devil's Arse, the oldest lead mine in Derbyshire and disappearing roads.

Distance     10 miles      Time      4 - 5 hours

Maps     OS Explorer OL1

Refreshments     Pubs, shops and cafés at Edale and Castleton.

Terrain     Field paths and quiet lanes lead across the Vale of Edale before a track (Chapel Gate) climbs up onto Rushup Edge. A boggy footpath then heads across Rushup Edge (narrow ridge in places) then down to join the road at the foot of Mam Tor. Field paths then lead across Treak Cliff (steep hillside) to reach Castleton. From Castleton, field paths lead up to join the former A625 from where a muddy path slants up to reach Hollins Cross on the Great Ridge. A rough path then drops down to join a track near Hollins Farm that leads down to join the valley road. Field paths lead back to Edale.

Ascents     Rushup Edge - 545 metres above sea level.
Hollins Cross - 390 metres above sea level.

Caution     The climb up onto Rushup Edge follows a steep, rough track. The path along the top of Rushup Edge has steep drops to the side of the path in places, whilst the narrow path across Treak Cliff traverses a steep hillside. The climb over the Great Ridge is also steep in places.

Barber Booth is a delightful hamlet of old cottages and farms as well as Edale Methodist Chapel, a simple building with attractive sash windows. The railway skirts just to the north of this hamlet before entering the two-mile long Cowburn Tunnel that burrows 800-ft beneath the moors en route from Sheffield to Manchester. Completed in the 1890's by the Midland Railway, it was designed to compete with the older trans-Pennine route through Longdendale and was instrumental in bringing visitors to Edale. From Barber Booth a track known as Chapel Gate heads up onto the broad ridge of Rushup Edge, with stunning views back across the head of the valley towards Kinder Scout. This was once the main road over to Chapel-en-le-Frith; 'gate' is the old Scandinavian word for road. Chapel Gate joins another old route along the top of Rushup Edge, with far-reaching views south across the White Peak and Chapel-en-le-Frith far below. Up here, only 200 yards of soggy moorland separates water flowing into the Irish Sea or the North Sea. The bridleway along the top of Rushup Edge has been in use since prehistoric times, the highlight of which is the Bronze Age burial mound of Lord's Seat where the ridge suddenly narrows and falls steeply away into the Vale of Edale.

Mam Tor stands at the dividing point between the Dark and White Peak. The limestone hills of Treak Cliff and Long Cliff were formed 350 million years ago as a reef in a warm tropical sea. Since Roman times, these hills have been mined for lead and the semi-precious Blue John stone. Levels were driven into the hillsides and natural caverns opened up, four of which are open today as show caves. A tour of the Blue John Cavern reveals a labyrinth of natural caverns as well as old mine workings where veins of Blue John can be seen sandwiched between the limestone rock. These veins are still worked by miners and the Blue John is crafted into jewellery and ornaments. Blue John is only found in the hill of Treak Cliff; a purple, yellow and white-banded fluorspar that got its name from the French words 'bleu jaune' meaning blue and yellow. It is said that Blue John vases were found amongst the ruins of Pompeii, although it was particularly popular in Georgian and Victorian times. A narrow path leads from Blue John Cavern across a steep hillside to reach Treak Cliff Cavern, which also has rich deposits of Blue John amongst a cave system that is renowned for its stalactites and stalagmites. Situated at the foot of Winnats Pass, Speedwell Cavern involves a boat journey along a flooded level through the workings of a 200-year-old lead mine to reach underground cave and river systems. Peak Cavern is the final sl ow cave, hidden in a dramatic gorge behind Castleton. The entrance to this cavern is awe-inspiring, a huge yawning hole that so frightened our ancestors that they thought it was the entrance to hell, hence its other name of the Devil's Arse! This is the largest cave entrance in the British Isles, where a community of ropemakers once lived and worked during the 18th and 19th Centuries making ropes for the local lead mines, as the damp atmosphere provided perfect conditions. The last ropemaker in Castleton retired in 1973. Beyond, the tour takes you for half a mile deep underground through the caverns.

Odin Mine is the oldest mine in Derbyshire, first mentioned in 1280 although the name suggests pre-Conquest origins as it is dedicated to the Norse god of wisdom, war and death. Situated at the foot of Mam Tor, the overgrown workings of this disused lead mine are fascinating with spoil heaps and a crushing wheel still in situ where the ore was sorted, crushed and washed. To the west of the road a narrow gorge leads to the mine entrance from where a maze of inter-connected levels reaches deep underground - *do not explore these dangerous workings*. From here, a path climbs up along the former A625, which famously slipped down the mountainside in 1979, before slanting up to reach Hollins Cross on the Great Ridge, once an important crossroads of packhorse trails from where there is a wonderful view across the Vale of Edale.

*For more information about Castleton, Mam Tor*
*and the Great Ridge, see Walking Weekend 3*

# EDALE SATURDAY WALK

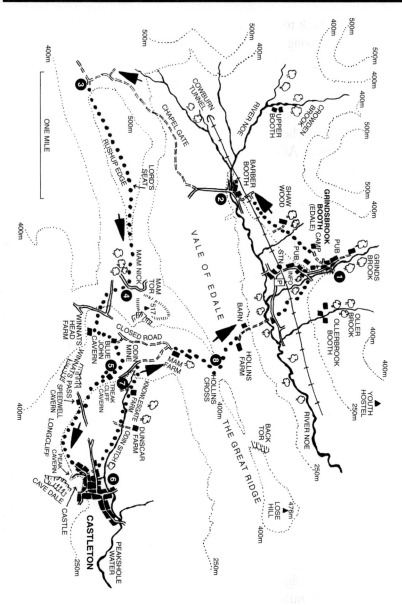

# THE WALK

*1.* With your back to the Old Nag's Head in the centre of Edale, head to the right along the track beside the 'phone box up through New Fold Farm and follow it bearing up to the left passing the Post Office and General Store towards Coopers Campsite then, where the track forks, carry straight on along the enclosed track out of the village. Follow this track straight on then, as you approach the gate at the top of the track just before the large barn, head left (SP) through a small gate in a fence. After the gate, bear right across the field to join the field boundary on the other side and follow this straight on across fields through three small gates (keeping the field boundary on your left) to reach a small wooded stream. Cross the stream and head out onto the field where you bear slightly left down over a farm track to reach a small gate at the bottom of the field (Shaw Wood Farm across to your right). After the gate, head straight on over the farm track and cross a FB over a stream then through a small gate that leads out onto a field. After the gate, head left for a few paces alongside the fence then turn right straight across the field down to reach a small gate in a fence on the opposite side. Head through the gate, and walk straight on alongside the fence on your left across several fields through a succession of small gates to join a rough track, which you follow straight on to join an enclosed track to the right of a railway bridge. Turn left over the bridge to join a lane at Barber Booth. Turn right along the lane and follow it curving left to reach the main road just above the bridge across the River Noe.

*2.* Turn right along the road down over the bridge then follow the road climbing straight up the hillside towards Chapel-en-le-Frith ('1-in-6' hill) for just over 0.25 miles then, just before the road bends left, take the track to the right through a gate. Follow this rough track (Chapel Gate) climbing steadily up at first then the track levels out and leads through two gates, after which it begins its long climb up onto Rushup Edge. Follow this rough track climbing up to reach a gate after 0.25 miles *(and a short level section to catch your breath)*, after which continue up along the track for a further 0.25 miles to the top of the climb. As you reach the top of the climb, the track passes a FP off to the right towards 'Upper Booth, Hayfield' just after which the gradient eases and the track curves round to the left and heads gently up onto the top of the broad moorland ridge of Rushup Edge. Continue along the track across the top of the moor, bending quite sharply round to the left (ignore the rough track off to the right) then straight on to reach a wall and track across your path (SP 'Castleton & Hope via Mam Tor, Hollins Cross').

3. Turn left along the path alongside the wall on your right and follow this straight on gently rising up for almost 1 mile up across the broad ridge to reach Lord's Seat on the rounded summit of Rushup Edge with a 'surprise view' across the Vale of Edale ahead (*the ridge narrows distinctly from this point onwards*). Carry straight on heading across the much narrower ridge gradually dropping down for a further 0.75 miles (*steep drops to the side of the path in places*). As you approach the end of this ridge (with hummocks down to your left and Mam Tor just ahead), drop down to the right slightly to join a broad bridleway which you follow straight on along the right-hand side of the narrow ridge down to join a fence/woodland on your right that leads through a gate to join the road at Mam Nick (*just below Mam Tor*).

4. Turn left up along the road to quickly reach a sharp bend where you turn right down some steps through a small gate (SP 'Cave Dale, Peak Forest'), after which head straight on along the grassy path down to reach the main road. Cross the road through the gate opposite to the left (SP) and follow the wide grassy path ahead for a few paces then follow the path bearing to the left to quickly re-join the road. Cross over the road through the wall-gate opposite and head straight on bearing very slightly to the left passing to the left side of the farm buildings, through a small wall-gate after which head alongside the wall on your right. When you are parallel to the farm buildings turn left across the field (SP 'Blue John Cavern') along a grassy path and follow this passing to the right above an area of low marshy ground then bearing round to the right to reach the entrance to Blue John Cavern. Pass in front of the building and head straight on through the gate ahead (*do not head down the driveway*), after

which head straight on across the field to reach another gate at the top of a steep bank. Follow the narrow path down across the steep hillside *(take care)* then curving round to the right across Treak Cliff to reach Treak Cliff Cavern.

5. Pass above the cavern buildings and down the steps to reach the viewing area beside the entrance. Head down the steps along the concrete path then, halfway down this path just before a bench, head through a gap in the railings on your right. Follow the grassy path running parallel with the concrete path at first then, where the concrete path bends down towards the road, carry straight on alongside a tumbledown wall on your left. Follow the path alongside this wall and through a wall-gate after which carry on to reach the road at the foot of Winnats Pass near the entrance to Speedwell Cavern. Cross the road through the gate opposite (National Trust sign 'Longcliff') and follow the path straight on keeping close to the wall on your left and follow this wall curving gradually round to the left (following the curve of the hillside) to eventually reach a gate at the start of a walled track on the edge of Castleton. Follow this track straight on down into Castleton, over Goosehill Bridge across Peakshole Water then straight into the Market Place beside the Youth Hostel. Turn left passing the George Inn to reach the main road.

6. Turn left along this main road to quickly reach a mini-roundabout beside the Castleton Centre where you carry straight on passing the Methodist Church and the path to Peak Cavern just after which turn right up steps along a narrow path between the houses (SP). Follow this path straight on to quickly reach a small gate that leads out onto a field where you bear left alongside the field boundary to reach a squeeze-stile, after which head straight on alongside the wooded stream on your right (Odin Sitch) across two fields to reach a farm track and bridge across the stream. At the bridge, carry straight on (SP 'Mam Tor, Odin Mine') across the field alongside the stream/fence on your right then, as you reach the top of this field, head over a small bridge and stile to your right then over a wall-stile after which head straight up across the field to reach a lane at the entrance to Knowlegates Farm.

7. At the lane in front of the farm, carry straight on (SP 'Mam Tor') along the path bearing round to the right through a small gate, up steps and over a stile. After the stile, follow the path to the left up across rough ground, over a stile and up to reach the overgrown workings of Odin Mine. Follow the path straight on then round to the left through some trees and over Odin Sitch passing the former crushing wheel and up to join a road (former A625). Turn right up along the road, which soon becomes a single lane road (*road closed due to subsidence*) then, just as the road bends sharp left through a bridle-gate across the road, take the FP to the right through a small gate in a fence beside the entrance to Mam Farm. Head through the gate and follow the clear but muddy path straight on rising up above Mam Farm then heading across the steep hillside passing above some cottages, after which the path slants steeply up to reach the path along the top of the Great Ridge at Hollins Cross (circular memorial).

8. At Hollins Cross, head straight on over the ridge and follow the wide path to the left heading steeply down the hillside into the Vale of Edale then, where the path forks after about 100 yards, follow the right-hand path (SP 'Edale') down across the hillside to reach a small gate in a wall just to the left of Hollins Farm. Head though the gate and drop down to join the farm lane, which you follow to the left down across fields to reach a bridge across the River Noe. Continue along the lane over the bridge then, as you approach the road, head up over the stile ahead to join the road. At the road, head through the small gate opposite and walk up the field alongside the wall on your left then, three-quarters of the way up the field, head left through a squeeze-stile. After the squeeze-stile, head diagonally to the right across the field to join a track that leads beneath a railway bridge, after which head straight on along the grassy track up to reach a gate in the field corner. Do not head through this gate but turn left immediately before it through a squeeze-stile then bear right across the field to reach another stile just to the right of a stone barn. After this stile, head straight on across the field (flagged path at first) to reach a gate and a track in the top left corner of the field. Head left through this gate and follow the lane over a bridge across Grinds Brook and up to join the road through Edale. Turn right back to the Old Nag's Head.

# Edale Walking Weekend
## - Sunday Walk -
### Edale, Kinder Scout, the Woolpacks, Edale Cross & Jacob's Ladder

## WALK INFORMATION

| | |
|---|---|
| Highlights | Ringing Roger, the dramatic ravine of Grindsbrook Clough, Kinder Scout plateau, wonderful weathered shapes, a moorland cross and a ladder down from the hills. |
| Distance | 8.5 miles      Time      4 hours |
| Maps | OS Explorer OL1 |
| Refreshments | Pubs, shops and cafés at Edale. Café at Upper Booth (seasonal). No other facilities en route - take plenty of provisions with you. |
| Terrain | A steep climb along rough paths leads up onto the escarpment of Kinder Scout. Rough, boggy paths then follow this edge all the way to join a track at Edale Cross. A steep path leads down Jacob's Ladder to Upper Booth from where field paths lead back to Edale. |
| Ascents | Kinder Scout - 620 metres above sea level. |
| Caution | This walk involves a long and steep climb up onto the plateau of Kinder Scout with an equally long and steep descent via Jacob's Ladder. There are sheer cliffs and steep drops to the side of the path along the edge of the escarpment. Navigation may be difficult in poor weather; map and compass essential. |
| Open Access | The path up to Kinder Scout and along the edge of the escarpment heads across Open Access land. See local signs for information or visit www.openaccess.gov.uk |

From Grindsbrook Booth, where several packhorse trails once converged, a steep climb leads up passing the outcrops of Ringing Roger (derived from the French word for rocks) onto the edge of the vast summit plateau of Kinder Scout, an incredible landscape of blanket bog and deep gullies that rarely dips below 600 metres. Shattered gritstone edges run all the way around this moorland plateau falling steeply away into the Woodlands Valley, Edale, Sett Valley and Ashop Clough. One of the most popular walking areas in Britain, it is a dangerous place with a morass of peat bogs dissected by a maze of deep groughs that will sap your energy and challenge even the most competent navigator. The blanket bog that covers Kinder Scout is 7,000 years old, a unique habitat formed when Stone Age people began to clear woodland thus creating wet conditions that allowed peat to form. This fragile landscape is home to sheep, grouse, curlew and mountain hare. It is also prone to erosion through pollution, over grazing and too many boots.

The exhilarating path along the southern edge of this plateau skirts the deep cleft of Grindsbrook Clough punctuated by rocky ravines and gritstone outcrops. Beyond Crowden Clough lie the Woolpacks, an amazing cluster of rocks weathered into weird and wonderful shapes. These gritstone outcrops are said to resemble the round packs of wool once carried by packhorses and some have names such as the Pagoda, Pym Chair or Moat Stone. Beyond the Woolpacks stands the isolated anvil-shaped Noe Stool, which lies close to the source of the River Noe with superb views ahead towards Edale Rocks. An old packhorse route between Hayfield and Edale is joined beside Edale Cross. This wayside cross dates back to medieval times and was used to mark the meeting point of three boundaries in the Royal Forest of the Peak. The track was used by packhorses carrying salt and cotton from Derbyshire and Yorkshire over to Lancashire and Cheshire in exchange for lead and coal. Our route follows this old packhorse trail down from the hills, with an exciting section known as Jacob's Ladder that drops steeply down to reach a packhorse bridge across the River Noe. This path takes its name from Jacob Marshall, an 18th Century farmer who cut steps into the hillside to ease the climb.

# EDALE SUNDAY WALK

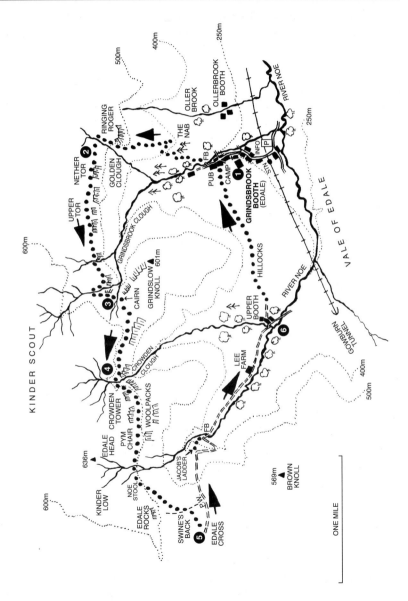

# THE WALK

1. Leave Grindsbrook Booth (Edale) along the lane to the left of the Old Nag's Head and follow this up heading out of the village (lane becomes a stony track) to reach a gate across the track beside a cottage where you follow the path down to the right (SP 'Grindsbrook') over a FB and up some steps out onto a field. Follow the flagged path to the left then, just by a small barn on your left, bear right along a grassy path slanting up the hillside to reach a bridlegate beside a plantation. Head through the gate, then follow the pitched-stone path steeply up to the right then, halfway up this plantation, follow the path bending sharp left climbing up across the hillside then sharp right up to reach the promontory of The Nab. Follow the path bending sharp left then gently rising up, with Grindsbrook Clough falling away to your left, to reach a fork in the path just before the outcrops of Ringing Roger. Bear left skirting around the base of these outcrops then round to the right heading up through the side-valley of Golden Clough to reach a large cairn just below the flat summit plateau. Just above this cairn, follow the clear rocky path to the left over a stream and up along a flagged path bearing to the left up onto the top of the gritstone edge of Nether Tor.

2. From Nether Tor, follow the clear path straight on along the edge of the plateau (stone-flagged path), with superb views down to your left, for just over 0.5 miles then gently rising up onto the outcrops of Upper Tor. Carry straight on across these outcrops then continue straight on along the plateau edge for a further 0.5 miles to reach the deep ravine of the eastern fork of the upper reaches of Grindsbrook Cough where you follow the path bending to the right to reach the head of this rocky ravine. Cross the stream/rocky ravine and follow the narrow path to the left along the other side of the ravine following the edge of the plateau again then round to the right to reach the head of another steep rocky ravine (the western fork of Grindsbrook Clough) where you join the eroded Grindsbrook path at a large cairn.

3. At the head of this ravine, bear very slightly to the left passing to the left side of the large cairn to quickly join a flagged path - follow this straight on across moorland (away from Grindsbrook Clough) to soon join the plateau edge again. Follow the wide path straight on along the edge for 0.5 miles to reach the head of Crowden Clough.

4. Cross the rocky stream then follow the eroded path straight on (just down from the fork in the stream) climbing steeply up the bank at first then bearing slightly left rising gently to reach the large gritstone outcrops of Crowden Tower. Continue along the clear eroded path to soon reach the strange outcrops of the Woolpacks. Follow the path through these scattered outcrops gently rising up to reach the Pym Chair (large outcrop) at the end of the Woolpacks where a stone-flagged path leads straight on across boggy peat hags (still following the edge of the plateau) to reach the isolated anvil-shaped outcrop of Noe Stool (Edale Rocks in the distance). At Noe Stool, follow the path bearing slightly to the left along the edge of the plateau dropping gently down for 0.5 miles alongside a tumbledown wall to reach a large cairn at the junction with the Pennine Way (Edale Rocks up to your right). Carry straight on along the pitched-stone path for a short distance then, where the path bends down to the left, carry straight on alongside an old wall on your left skirting below Swine's Back to soon reach another wall across your path. Turn left down to reach a gate that leads onto a clear track beside Edale Cross.

5. Turn left along this track and follow it steadily dropping down for 0.75 miles to reach a large cairn at the brow of a steep hill at the top of Jacob's Ladder (footpath). Follow the pitched-stone path to the left snaking down to reach the Packhorse Bridge across the River Noe. Cross the bridge then follow the track straight on down the valley to reach Lee Farm. Head through the farmyard then follow the lane down into the hamlet of Upper Booth.

6. As you reach the 'phone box in the centre of Upper Booth turn left (SP 'Edale') and follow the track bending to the right through the yard of Upper Booth Farm then round to the left then, where the track forks, follow the right-hand enclosed track towards 'Edale' (SP 'Pennine Way'). Follow this stony track straight on through a gate,

after which follow the path bending to the left then gently rising up, through old stone gateposts then a small gate in a fence after which continue up passing a ruinous barn to reach a stile over a fence. After the stile, bear very slightly to the right up passing between the hillocks (landslip) to reach a wall-gate at the top of the small hill. Follow the clear stone-flagged path straight on, with Vale of Edale before you, through a series of bridle-gates and stiles for just over 0.5 miles to join a tree-shaded track, which you follow to the right (SP 'Edale') down alongside a stream back to Grindsbrook Booth.

*Edale*

# EYAM

*Eyam (pronounced 'Eem') is one of the most famous villages in England due to the altruism of its inhabitants during the 17th Century when it was gripped by an outbreak of plague. Disease was a fact of life in medieval England; what sets Eyam apart is the tale of selfless heroism. In September 1665 a box of cloth arrived from London for local tailor George Viccars who was lodging with the Hadfield family in a house near the church. The cloth was damp and so he laid it out in front of the fire to dry. Unbeknownst to him, the cloth was home to plague-infected fleas. Within days he had died, and within a few weeks several other villagers had also died. Panic spread and some people began to flee the village. Fearing the infection would spread to neighbouring villages, the local Rector William Mompesson along with the Non-Conformist preacher Thomas Stanley, asked the villagers to voluntarily quarantine themselves. Food and supplies were left at the parish boundary stones dotted on the outskirts of the village where money was left in vinegar-filled holes in return for the supplies. The church was closed and open-air services were held in the wooded limestone valley of Cucklet Delf just to the south of the village; families buried their dead in fields near their houses. By the time the Plague ended in October 1666, around 260 people had died out of a village population of 350, although the two ministers were amongst the survivors. Despite the terrible loss, their efforts were successful and the disease did not spread. Information plaques around the village bring this incredibly moving tale of self-sacrifice to life; the solitary graves dotted around the fields are particularly poignant.*

## THE VILLAGE

Eyam is a busy tourist village with plenty of B&B's, the Miners' Arms, Youth Hostel, tea shops, general stores, craft shops, bakers, butcher's shop, Post Office, car park, toilets, bus service, Tourist Information Point, Eyam Museum, Eyam Hall and lots of historic buildings associated with the Plague.

## ACCOMMODATION

Tourist Information Centre, Bakewell:     01629 816558

## EYAM PUB

**Miners' Arms, Eyam:**                    **01433 630853**
Tucked away off The Square in the heart of the village, this whitewashed pub was built 35 years before the Plague struck and is reputedly haunted. Inside this traditional village pub there is a bar, lounge and dining room with beams and stone fireplaces.

## PUBS ALONG THE WALKS

Barrel Inn, Bretton:              01433 630856
Bull's Head Inn, Foolow:          01433 630873
Moon Inn, Stoney Middleton:       01433 630203
White Lion, Great Longstone:      01629 640252
Crispin Inn, Great Longstone:     01629 640237

# Eyam Walking Weekend
## - Saturday Walk -
### Eyam, Stoney Middleton, Coombs Dale
### & Longstone Edge

## WALK INFORMATION

| | |
|---|---|
| Highlights | The vinegar-filled stone, Roman baths, secluded Coombs Dale, deep quarries, a fine moorland edge and some delightful White Peak villages. |
| Distance | 11 miles      Time      5 hours |
| Maps | OS Explorer OL24 |
| Refreshments | Pubs and/or shops and cafés at Eyam, Stoney Middleton and Great Longstone. Pub at Foolow. |
| Terrain | A mixture of field paths, rough tracks, country lanes and moorland paths, with a number of ascents/descents. |
| Ascents | High Rake - 350 metres above sea level<br>Longstone Moor - 385 metres above sea level |
| Caution | This walk includes a number of steep sections. Keep well away from any quarry workings. Take care when crossing or walking along roads. |

# POINTS OF INTEREST

Eyam is a delightful place to explore with attractive houses and interesting corners including Eyam Hall, a fine manor house built in 1676 and still the family home of the Wright family. St Lawrence's Church occupies a religious site dating back to Saxon times; note the 8th Century preaching cross in the churchyard, the finest in Derbyshire. The present church dates from the 12th Century and boasts rare 16th Century wall paintings, a cupboard made from the clothier's box that brought the plague to Eyam, a Plague Register showing the monthly death tolls as well as Mompesson's chair. In the churchyard are several interesting graves, including that of Catherine, wife of William Mompesson, who died from the Plague. Eyam was one of the first places in England to have a public water supply when a network of water troughs were erected throughout the village in 1558 supplied by springs flowing down from Eyam Edge. These provided the village water supply for over 350 years; 'eyam' comes from the Saxon words meaning 'village by the water'. This quiet village was once a hive of industrial activity with lead mining, cotton spinning, silk weaving and shoe making - the last shoe manufacturer closed in 1979! From The Square in the centre of the village, a narrow lane leads out of Eyam known as Lydgate. This was once the main road to Stoney Middleton where an armed 'watch and ward' guard would keep an eye on who was coming into the village during the hours of darkness. The lane passes the Lydgate Graves of plague victims George Darby and his daughter Mary set in a small enclosure. Midway between Eyam and Stoney Middleton on the parish boundary stands the famous Boundary Stone where money was left during the Plague in vinegar filled holes in exchange for provisions.

Stoney Middleton is a jumble of winding lanes sheltered in the wooded valley of Middleton Dale, which is sadly scarred by large quarries and a busy road. Tucked away along The Nook are two unusual buildings. St Martin's Church was built by Joan Eyre in the 15th Century as thanksgiving for the return of her husband from the Battle of Agincourt. The tower remains, although an unusual octagonal lantern nave was added in the 18th Century that gives the church a strange appearance. Just beyond the church are the Roman Baths. There is little evidence to support the theory that the Romans used this thermal spring, as its first recorded use was in the Middle Ages. The spring became popular in the 18th Century when Dr Short suggested drinking the water to help cure rheumatism and 'saltness of blood'. In the early 19th Century, the bath was covered over and changing rooms built, however, as the popularity of spa cures waned the baths fell into disrepair; they were restored during the 1980's.

From Stoney, a path heads over into steep-sided Coombs Dale with its rushing stream muddied from quarry workings. The Sallet Hole Mine was operational until a few years ago producing quality fluorspar used in the steel industry. The fenced off flooded mine level cuts deep into the hillside, although nature is reclaiming the landscape with a profusion of wild flowers in spring and wooded hillsides. Above this valley is a vast quarry that stretches along much of Longstone Edge - the scale of quarrying is an eye-opener! The High Rake quarry is particularly striking with deep yet narrow workings right next to the road. The end product of all of this devastation is fluorspar, as well as an irreversible scar in the heart of one of our National Parks!

Sheltered beneath this escarpment is Great Longstone, a delightful cluster of cottages, pubs, church and farms set around a small tree-shaded green complete with stepped market cross. It was the mineral deposits, particularly lead, along the escarpment of Longstone Edge to the north of the village that brought prosperity to Great Longstone, although the name of one of the village inns reminds us of another local trade for St Crispin is the patron saint of cobblers. This escarpment stretches for five miles through the heart of the Peak District. Its western end is least scarred by quarrying and the views from Longstone Moor back across Great Longstone towards the wooded undulating hills around Bakewell and the Wye Valley are superb. To the north, the long descent towards Foolow reveals a far-reaching view towards Mam Tor, Kinder Scout and Derwent Edge.

*For more information about Foolow, see Sunday Walk*

# EYAM SATURDAY WALK

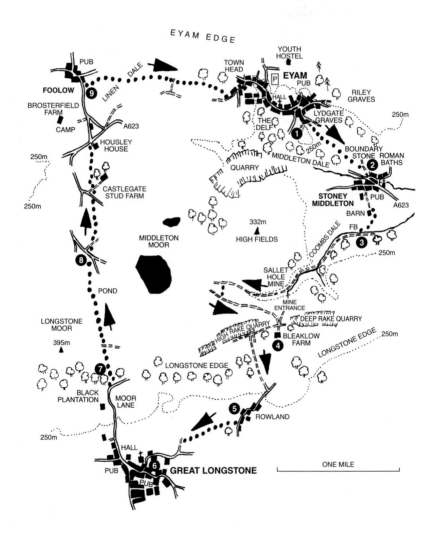

# THE WALK

1. From The Square in the centre of Eyam (with your back to Water Lane and the Miners' Arms), head straight on along Lydgate and follow this passing the Lydgate Graves then, where the lane forks on the edge of Eyam (Mill Lane off to your left), head straight on along the walled track (SP 'Stoney Middleton, Boundary Stone') through two gates and out onto a field. Follow the track across two fields to reach a squeeze-stile beside a gate that leads onto an enclosed path (SP 'Stoney Middleton, Boundary Stone'). Walk straight on along this path to soon reach another squeeze-stile at the end of the enclosed path, after which carry straight on across the field to reach the Boundary Stone set in the middle of the field above a steep bank (The Cliff). Continue straight on bearing slightly to the right down the steep hillside to join a lane on the outskirts of Stoney Middleton.

2. Turn right down along the lane into the village then, at the foot of Cliff Bottom, follow the lane to the left down through the village then round to the right up to reach the main road (A623) opposite the Moon Inn. Take the road opposite (High Street) and follow this steeply up through the village then turn left along Eton Fold ('leading to Vicarage Lane'). Follow this lane straight on out of the village (lane becomes a track after the last houses) - continue along this track passing a house on your right ('Janesway') just after which you reach a gate at the end of the track (to the left of the driveway leading to another house). Head through this gate (waymarker) and follow the grassy track straight on across two fields then, where the track forks beside some barns, head left over a stile (SP 'Coombs Dale'). After the stile, turn sharp right to quickly reach a stile over a fence about 25 yards to the left of the barns (ignore stile at bottom of field). Cross this stile and head straight on across the field gently curving to the right then steeply down the hillside through gorse bushes to reach a plank FB across a muddy stream at the bottom of Coombs Dale to join a lane just beyond.

3. Turn right and follow this lane heading up through wooded Coombs Dale with the stream on your right. After 0.5 miles the lane crosses the stream and climbs up a bank then bends round to the right and levels out (valley opens out). Continue straight on along the track heading up along the valley floor passing the former Sallet Hole Mine after 0.25 miles, after which carry on along the track heading up through the valley (stream now flows down the track) for almost 0.75 miles to reach a FP across the track (SP on right-hand side of track). Turn left over the stile and head straight up the valley side, over a tumbledown wall across your path then continue up across the rough hillside to reach a walled track across your path. Turn left along this track and follow it gently rising up *(views across Coombs Dale after a while)* for 0.5 miles to reach a junction of tracks/paths beside the quarry entrance (High Rake) where you head straight on through a bridlegate beside a double metal gate that leads onto a stony lane (opposite entrance to Bleaklow Farm).

4. Turn right up along the track with the deep quarry on your right then, where the track bends round to the right (deepest part of the quarry on your right) turn left along a walled stony track (ignore the track immediately before this). Follow this walled track heading steadily down across Longstone Edge for 0.5 miles to reach a lane at the bottom of the track. Turn right along this lane into Rowland.

5. Follow the road down through Rowland then, as you reach the last houses on your left (postbox and Rake's Barn), turn right through a squeeze-stile (SP). Head alongside the wall on your right then, where this wall bends away after a short distance, continue straight on across the field to reach a wall-stile. After the wall-stile, bear slightly left across the field to reach a squeeze-stile between the barn and the gate in the bottom left field corner (yellow marker). After this squeeze-stile, head straight on alongside the wall on your left to reach another squeeze-stile in the field corner, after which head straight down across two fields to join a walled grassy path. Turn left to reach the road on the outskirts of Great Longstone. Turn right along the road and follow it into the village to reach a T-junction opposite the White Lion.

6. Turn right along the road up through the village passing the green and then the Crispin Inn (heading towards 'Little Longstone') then, where the road bends left, take the turning to the right along Moor Lane towards 'Longstone Edge'. Follow this lane out of the village rising steadily up for 0.75 miles then, where it bends right at the foot of the wooded Longstone Edge, head straight on through a gate (SP 'Longstone Edge and Wardlow') that leads into Black Plantation. Follow the path up through the woods, over a track and up some steps - the path slants to the right across the wooded hillside then climbs steeply up to reach a gate in a fence at the top of the woods (Longstone Moor ahead).

7. Head through the gate and follow the path rising up across the heather moorland onto the top of the moor - carry straight on across the moor passing a small but deep fenced-off quarry to reach an old quarry track just beyond. Cross over the track and carry straight on along the grassy path (passing a solitary hawthorn tree) heading up onto the top of the next rise (SP 'Foolow' on the brow of the hill) - continue straight on along the path gradually dropping down across the moorland to reach a wall-stile at the bottom of the moor to the left of a dew pond. Cross the stile and bear slightly right across the field and over a wall-stile, after which carry straight on across two more fields to join a road.

8. Take the FP opposite through a wall-gate (SP) and bear slightly left across the field, over a tumbledown wall and on to reach a wall-gate that leads onto a track. Cross the stile opposite, then head to the right and follow the path across several fields over a series of stiles (heading towards Castlegate Stud Farm ahead) to join a road two fields before the farm. Cross the road through the squeeze-stile opposite (SP) and bear left to reach a wall-stile towards the field corner that leads onto the farm lane where you cross the stile opposite. After the stile, head straight on across the field and follow the field bending round to the right to reach a stile beside a gate in the far corner. After the stile, follow the path straight on across the field and over a wall-stile, after which head down across the field to reach a gate in the bottom right corner. After the gate, head straight

on to join a track that leads towards Houseley House Farm - as you reach the farmyard (dew pond to your left) follow the path skirting to the left of the farmyard (do not enter farmyard) to reach the A623 beside the farm entrance. Cross the main road and follow the road opposite towards 'Foolow', bearing left at the next junction into Foolow.

9. As you reach the '30 mph' sign on the edge of Foolow, take the FP to the right over a stile beside a gate that leads through the yard of a house (barn conversion) and over another stile out onto a field. Head straight on through the small gate (SP), then bear left through another small gate after which carry on across two more fields to join the bottom of a rough walled track beside a ruinous barn. Head straight over the track and follow the path alongside the wall on your right over wall-stiles and down into the shallow valley of Linen Dale. Head through the squeeze-stile at the bottom of the valley (SP 'Eyam'), then bear slightly left up the grassy bank, over a tumbledown wall and on across the next field to reach a wall-gate (SP). After this wall-gate, head straight on across the field and through another wall-gate, after which carry straight on across the next field over a tumbledown wall across your path then continue on alongside a wall on your right to reach a wall-gate beside a gate in the field corner that leads onto a walled track. At the track, head through the squeeze-stile opposite and follow the path across several fields over a further five stiles *(Eyam comes into view after the fifth stile)*. Continue straight on gradually dropping down the hillside alongside the wall on your right and through a squeeze-stile in the bottom right corner of the field, after which follow the path straight on across three more fields then along a narrow path between some houses to join Tideswell Lane on the outskirts of Eyam. Turn left along this lane down to join the main road at Town Head where you turn right back into Eyam.

# Eyam Walking Weekend
# - Sunday Walk -
## Eyam Moor, Bretton Clough,
## the Barrel Inn & Foolow

## WALK INFORMATION

| | |
|---|---|
| Highlights | The Plague Village, fine views from Eyam Edge, Sir William's road, a wonderful trek across heather moorland, ancient woods and tumbling streams, the highest pub in Derbyshire and Peakland's prettiest village. |
| Distance | 7.5 miles          Time          3 hours |
| Maps | OS Explorer OL24 |
| Refreshments | Pub, shops and cafés at Eyam. Pubs at Bretton and Foolow. |
| Terrain | Field and woodland paths lead up onto Eyam Edge to join the walled track of Sir William Hill Road. A path then heads across Eyam Moor with a fairly steep descent to reach an escarpment above Bretton Clough from where a grassy track leads steadily down into the wooded confines of Bretton Clough. A path then leads up through this valley before a steep climb to reach the Barrel Inn. After a short section of road-walking, a track heads west then a path turns south across fields to reach Foolow from where field paths lead back to Eyam. |
| Ascents | Eyam Moor - 410 metres above sea level. Barrel Inn, Bretton - 385 metres above sea level. |
| Caution: | This walk involves several steep sections, particularly the climbs up onto Eyam Edge and out of Bretton Clough. The path across Eyam Moor and through Bretton Clough is muddy with some rocky sections. There are steep drops to the side of the path on the descent into Bretton Clough. |

# POINTS OF INTEREST

This walk heads up to join Sir William Hill Road that runs across the top of Eyam Edge, one-time packhorse route, salt-road and Turnpike Road that linked Sheffield with Buxton. Some historians believe this route has Roman origins. No one is sure just who Sir William was; perhaps it was William Peverel whose built his castle overlooking the Hope Valley just after the Conquest, or Sir William Cavendish of Chatsworth or even Sir William Saville, Lord of the Manor of Eyam. Beyond this ancient road lies Eyam Moor, a wonderful expanse of heather moorland with superb views in all directions, especially the 'surprise' view from the brow of a steep bank with Stanage Edge and Higger Tor rising up above the rooftops of Hathersage and the wooded Derwent Valley far below. This moorland is littered with Bronze Age burial mounds as well as a stone circle known as Wet Withens. A moorland path drops down to reach an abrupt escarpment above the wooded cleft of Bretton Clough, a delightful valley with trickling streams and steep hillsides cloaked in ancient woodland. From the hidden beauty spot of Stoke Ford at the confluence of Abney Clough and Bretton Clough, where five old packhorse trails converge, a path leads up through this delectable valley to reach the Barrel Inn at Bretton set on the crest of Eyam Edge. This is the highest pub in Derbyshire (1,275-ft) from where it is possible to see five English counties - the pub is situated slap bang in the middle of the Peak District with the gritstone moors of the Dark Peak to the north and the limestone plateau of the White Peak to the south. Dating back to 1597, the pub once served travellers along Sir William Hill Road during its turnpike days.

The attractive village of Foolow lies at the foot of the Edge, its delightful houses and chapels clustered around a village green complete with duck pond, enclosed well, 14th Century stepped cross and bull ring. The cross was originally a boundary marker of the Royal Forest of the Peak *(see Castleton for more details)*. The name of the village is derived from a Saxon farmer called 'Foo' who gave his name to a nearby hill or 'low' - and nothing to do with the local village idiot, although just to the west is a dry limestone valley called Silly Dale!

# EYAM SUNDAY WALK

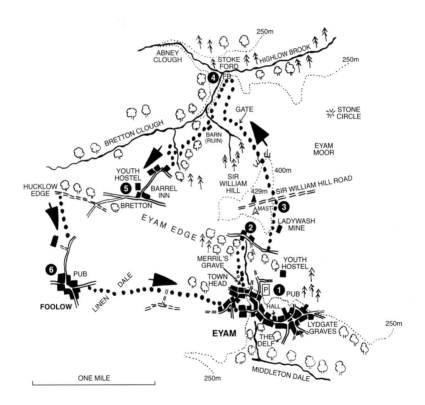

250m

ABNEY CLOUGH

STOKE FORD

HIGHLOW BROOK

250m

4 FB

GATE

STONE CIRCLE

BRETTON CLOUGH

BARN (RUIN)

EYAM MOOR

YOUTH HOSTEL

SIR WILLIAM HILL

400m

HUCKLOW EDGE

5 BARREL INN

BRETTON

429m SIR WILLIAM HILL ROAD

MAST 3

EYAM EDGE

LADYWASH MINE

2

MERRIL'S GRAVE

YOUTH HOSTEL

6 PUB

DALE

LINEN

TOWN HEAD

P 1 PUB

FOOLOW

HALL

EYAM

LYDGATE GRAVES

250m

THE DELF

ONE MILE

250m

MIDDLETON DALE

# THE WALK

1. From The Square in the centre of Eyam (with your back to Water Lane and the Miners' Arms), turn right up along Church Street and follow this through the village passing the church on your right then Eyam Hall. Continue along the road through the village passing Hawkhill Road and then the turning along Little Edge, just after which you pass Merrill House *(where plague victim Humphrey Merril died)* 25 yards after which turn right along a track between the houses (SP). Follow this track up to reach a gate at the top of the track on the edge of the village (SP), after which bear left up across the field *(Humphrey Merril's grave to your right)* to reach a small wall-gate in the top left corner just below a house. After the gate, follow the short section of enclosed path to the left to quickly reach the driveway beside the entrance to the house. Cross over this driveway and follow the enclosed grassy path opposite (house gardens on your right) up to a gate that leads out onto a field. After the gate, head to the right up across the field to join a wall on your right which you follow climbing quite steeply up the hillside. As you reach the top of the field you head up through an area of gorse/trees that quickly leads up into woodland where, after a short distance, you follow the path bending to the right up through woodland (Jumber Brook down to your right). The path leads up over the stream above a small waterfall then on to reach an enclosed stony track where you turn left up to quickly join the road along Eyam Edge.

2. Turn right along the road for about 300 yards then follow the road as it gently curves round to the left, just after which cross the wall-stile to the left (SP). After the wall-stile, head straight on up across the field alongside the wall on your right. After a while the field levels out (transmitter mast to your left) - continue straight on alongside the wall to reach a wall-stile in the field corner that leads onto the enclosed track of Sir William Hill Road.

3. Cross the wall-stile opposite (SP 'Stoke Ford') and follow the path straight on across Eyam Moor for 0.25 miles to reach the brow of a

steep bank beside a stone cairn *(superb views)*. Continue straight on along the clear path down the steep bank then gradually drop down across the moorland along a rocky path to reach a gate set in a narrow corner of the boundary wall at the bottom of Eyam Moor. Cross the stile beside the left-hand gate, after which follow the wide grassy path straight on alongside the wall on your right gently dropping down (steep escarpment to your left above Bretton Clough), passing some gritstone outcrops where the path curves round to the right (wall still on your right) down to reach another stile beside a gate. Head through the gate and continue along the wide grassy path gently dropping down then, after a while, the path gradually bears to the left away from the wall heading more steeply down across the hillside to reach the top of a steep wooded bank. Follow the path to the left across the top of this wooded bank then winding down to join a clear path just above Bretton Brook, with the FB of Stoke Ford just down to your right.

4. As you reach this clear path above Bretton Brook, turn left (away from Stoke Ford) across the steep wooded hillside (Bretton Brook down to your right) through gorse and trees to reach a stile in a wall. Cross the stile and continue straight on across the sparsely wooded hillside then follow the path round to the left into a wooded side-valley to reach an old bridge across a small stream. Cross the bridge and follow the path heading straight on up a grassy bank passing below the ruins of Gotherage Barn. The path levels out and leads on across undulating fields crossing tumbledown walls before skirting the foot of a wooded bank (boggy ground) beyond which the path gently rises up to reach a fence and wooded ravine across your path. Follow the path to the left (alongside the ravine) up to reach a stile to the right that leads over the small stream. After the stream, follow the path ahead bending sharp left after a short distance climbing up across the steep wooded hillside (ravine to your left) before zig-zagging steeply up to reach a stile beside a gate (above the wooded ravine). Head over the stile and follow the enclosed path straight on to reach a road beside the houses of Nether Bretton. Turn right along the road rising gently up to reach a T-junction beside the Barrel Inn on the top of Eyam Edge.

5. Turn right along the road along the top of Eyam Edge for 250 yards then follow the road slanting down to the left (road-sign 'Foolow') across the wooded escarpment. Just after the road emerges from the woodland and curves round to the left at the foot of the escarpment, turn right along an enclosed rough track. Follow this straight on across the foot of the escarpment for just over 0.25 miles then take the FP to the left through a small gate in a section of fence (waymarker). After the stile, head down the grassy bank, at the bottom of which head through the (second) small gate to your right that leads out into the corner of a field. After the gate, head left alongside the wall on your left heading down across two fields to reach a wall-stile to your left about 75 yards before the bottom corner of the second field that leads onto a road. Turn right along the road into Foolow.

6. As you reach the road through Foolow (village green in front of you) turn left towards 'Eyam' passing the Bull's Head Inn and follow the road straight on out of the village towards 'Eyam, Grindleford'. Continue along the road for about 200 yards then, immediately after the Foolow village sign, take the FP to the right over a wall-stile (SP). Bear left across the field and through a squeeze-stile that leads onto the end of a rough walled track (beside a ruinous barn). Head straight over the track and follow the path alongside the wall on your right over wall-stiles and down into the shallow valley of Linen Dale. Head through the squeeze-stile at the bottom of the valley (SP 'Eyam'), then bear slightly left up the grassy bank, over a tumbledown wall and on across the next field to reach a wall-gate (SP). After this wall-gate, head straight on across the field and through another wall-gate, after which carry straight on across the next field over a tumbledown wall across your path then continue on alongside a wall on your right to reach a wall-gate beside a gate in the field corner that leads onto a walled track. At the track, head through the squeeze-stile opposite and follow the path across several fields over a further five stiles *(Eyam comes into view after the fifth stile)*. Continue straight on gradually dropping down the hillside alongside the wall on your right and through a squeeze-stile in the bottom right corner of the

field, after which follow the path straight on across three more fields then along a narrow path between some houses to join Tideswell Lane on the outskirts of Eyam. Cross the lane and follow the FP opposite (SP) straight on across the field to quickly join another lane, where you take the enclosed FP opposite to the right. Follow this down to emerge in a small housing development where you head straight on down to join the main road through Eyam. Turn right back to reach The Square.

*Eyam*

# HARTINGTON

*Hartington is a village of great charm with old cottages looking out across a spacious market place complete with duck pond, village green and a water pump built to commemorate the coronation of King Edward VII. Its history can be traced back to Norman times when it was recorded as 'Hortedun' in the Domesday Book (derived from a Saxon personal name and 'dun' meaning 'low hill'). Following the Conquest, the Manor of Hartington was granted to Henry De Ferrers whose family administered it for 200 years until their lands were forfeited to the Crown after rebelling against Henry III. The manor was subsequently given to Prince Edmund, the Earl of Lancaster, and later became part of the Duchy of Lancaster. In the 17th Century, it was bought by the Cavendish family of Chatsworth (Dukes of Devonshire), since when the Duke's eldest son has been given the title of Marquis of Hartington. During the time of the De Ferrers, Hartington grew into a bustling trading centre and became the first Peak village to be granted a market charter in 1203. The layout of the market place has changed little in over eight centuries – note the former Market Hall with its carved datestone of 1836. It was around this time that St Giles' Church was founded on a rise of land overlooking the market place, noted for its medieval gargoyles and imposing battlemented tower. Above the village stands Hartington Hall, a fine yeoman's manor house that was built in 1611 by the Bateman family who lived in the hall up until the 1930's when it became a Youth Hostel. Hartington is famous for cheese as this is one of the few places where Stilton is made in a creamery built by the Duke of Devonshire in the 1870's; Stilton can only be produced in the shires of Leicester, Nottingham and Derby. Sadly, Hartington Creamery – the last remaining Stilton cheese producer in Derbyshire – closed in 2009.*

## THE VILLAGE

Hartington boasts several B&B's, Youth Hostel, two coaching inns, general stores, cafés, newsagents, Post Office, the Old Cheese Shop, craft and gift shops, garage, bus service, car park, payphone and toilets.

## ACCOMMODATION

Tourist Information Centre, Ashbourne:     01335 343666

## HARTINGTON PUBS

**Devonshire Arms, Hartington:          01298 84232**
A pub of considerable charm and character overlooking the spacious market place with a traditional tap-room, cosy lounge warmed by an open fire and a separate dining room. No accommodation

**Charles Cotton Hotel, Hartington:       01298 84229**
This large, stone-built coaching inn dates back to the early 1800's when it was originally known as the Sleigh Arms after a notable local family. It retains much of its original layout with a low doorway leading through to the rear bar and lounge with its large stone fireplace.

## PUBS ALONG THE WALKS

The George, Alstonefield:              01335 310205
Staffordshire Knott, Sheen:            01298 84329

# Hartington Walking Weekend
## - Saturday Walk -
*Hartington, Biggin Dale, Wolfscote Dale,*
*Milldale & Alstonefield*

## WALK INFORMATION

| | |
|---|---|
| Highlights | The home of Stilton, five valleys in a day, National Nature Reserves, a famous packhorse bridge and the haunt of the Compleat Angler. |
| Distance | 10 miles          Time          5 hours |
| Maps | OS Explorer OL24 |
| Refreshments | Pubs at Hartington and Alstonefield. Shops and cafés at Hartington and Milldale. |
| Terrain | From Hartington, a walled track leads over to Biggin Dale from where a path heads down through this steep-sided valley across pastures, through woodland and along the rocky valley floor to reach its confluence with Wolfscote Dale. A riverside path then leads downstream to reach Lode Mill from where there is a steep climb up to Shining Tor and a high-level traverse before a steep descent to Milldale. A fairly steep climb leads up to Alstonefield. After some road walking, field paths/tracks lead down through Narrowdale to join a track which is followed down to join the riverside path through Beresford Dale. Field paths lead back to Hartington. |
| Ascents | Highfield Lane - 317 metres above sea level<br>Shining Tor - 250 metres above sea level |
| Caution | This walk involves several short but steep sections, with steep drops to the side of the path above Shining Tor. Take care along the roads around Alstonefield. |

Hartington nestles in the broad upper reaches of the River Dove, a valley of rich farmland and green hills. To the south lie a range of imposing limestone hills including Gratton Hill and Wolfscote Hill that mark a dramatic change of landscape where the shales and sandstones of the Dark Peak meet the White Peak limestone plateau. The River Dove has cut a narrow gorge through this limestone bedrock, a wonderful valley of towering crags and wooded slopes that stretches for several miles until it meets the River Manifold near the village of Ilam from where the river continues on its meandering journey to swell the waters of the River Trent. This is a beautiful world of hidden valleys, limestone outcrops and crystal-clear water. Each stretch of this gorge has its own name and character; our route takes in Beresford Dale, Wolfscote Dale and Mill Dale as well as the tributary of Biggin Dale, although Dovedale proper lies downstream of the hamlet of Milldale. These steep-sided valleys are the preserve of walkers who come to marvel at the landscape, a magical place for a walk especially in spring when wild flowers carpet the hillsides and birds dart amongst the trees.

Biggin Dale is a steep-sided valley that is dry for most of the year, although a stream reappears after heavy rain. It is a valley of real contrast with steep grassy slopes scarred by limestone scree and dotted with trees, whilst the middle section of the valley is preserved as a nature reserve with ancient woodland. The valley joins Wolfscote Dale beneath the towering outcrops of Peaseland Rocks, from where our route follows the gentle flow of the River Dove downstream to reach Lode Mill, one of the finest stretches of footpath in England. This river forms the boundary between Derbyshire (eastern side) and Staffordshire. Lead was once smelted at Lode Mill in the 18th and 19th Centuries, later converted to grind corn. The buildings have a delightful setting beside the river with the outcrops of Shining Tor rising above. Over a century ago there were a handful of mills along this stretch of valley, which is known as Mill Dale. The hamlet of Milldale lies just downstream of Lode Mill, a popular walking centre with a shop, information barn and 17th Century packhorse bridge across the Dove known as Viator's

Bridge, which marks the start of Dovedale proper. The name of this bridge comes from a character in Izaak Walton's book The Compleat Angler. There has been a mill in this village for centuries, although the last mill was derelict by the late 19th Century. Only a few remains can be seen of this old mill, which once produced ochre dyes from ironstone.

Alstonefield is a delightful village situated high on the limestone plateau between Dovedale and the Manifold Valley, first settled by a Saxon farmer called Aelfstan. Old cottages cluster around small greens with a fine country pub overlooking the larger tree-shaded green at the heart of the village. At its southern edge stands St Peter's Church. There has been a church on this site since the 9th Century, as the numerous broken Saxon carved stones and crosses around it testify. The present church dates mainly from the 12th to 15th Centuries with some Norman stonework. The church is noted for the ornate Cotton family pew and finely carved 17th Century double-decker pulpit. Alstonefield is still an agricultural village, as it has been for over 1,000 years, and is noted for the medieval open field strips surrounding the village that have been enclosed by walls thus 'fossilising' this historic farming pattern. From Alstonefield, a path leads through the hidden valley of Narrowdale that lies sandwiched between Narrowdale Hill and Gratton Hill, with superb views ahead across the upper Dove Valley.

Beresford Dale is the name given to the top section of the Dove gorge before it opens out into the broad valley around Hartington. It will forever be associated with Izaak Walton, who fished along this river with his friend Charles Cotton, poet and raconteur, who lived at Beresford Hall. Charles Cotton was an expert fly-fisherman who introduced Walton to the delights of the River Dove and tutored him on the art of fly-fishing. In 1653 Izaak Walton published The Compleat Angler, a literary classic that has the distinction of being the third most reprinted book in the English language! It also offers a rare insight into 17th Century English country life. Cotton penned a chapter on fly-fishing for Walton's 5th edition published in 1676. Beresford Hall was demolished in the 1850's but the 17th Century riverside 'fishing temple' survives where Walton and Cotton spent many happy hours.

*For more information about Dovedale, see Walking Weekend 11*

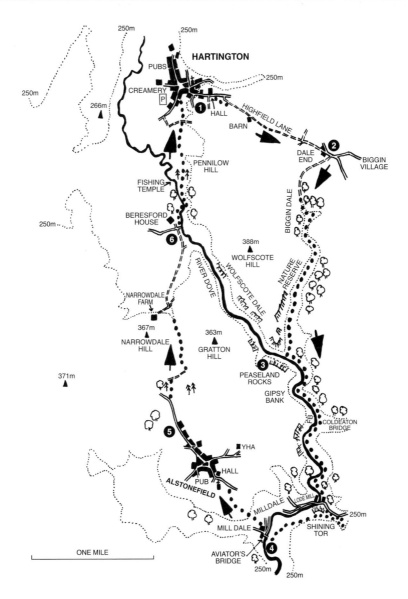

ONE MILE

# THE WALK

1. From the market square in the centre of Hartington (with your back to the Devonshire Arms), turn right along the road towards 'Ashbourne' then, after a short distance, turn right along Hall Bank and follow this climbing up to reach Hartington Hall (Youth Hostel) on the edge of the village. Carry straight on along the road then, about 50 yards after the Hall, take the FP to the right through a gate (SP). After the gate, head left across the field to quickly reach a squeeze-stile in a wall, after which follow the path straight on *(heading towards the barn ahead)* through another squeeze-stile then carry straight on alongside the walled track on your left to soon reach a stile to your left halfway up the field that leads onto this walled track. Turn right along the track (Highfield Lane) and follow it rising up passing the barn. Continue along the track as it gently rises up then levels out and gradually drops down (keep to the clear track) all the way to reach the road at Dale End beside some houses.

2. Turn right along the road for 50 yards then take the track to the right through a gate just before the turning to the left (National Trust sign 'Biggin Dale' & SP). Follow the track heading down into Biggin Dale along the valley floor then gently curving round to the left and over a wall-stile across your path. After the stile, carry straight on along the broad grassy path heading down the valley with a tumbledown wall on your left then, as you approach a side-valley to your left (where the valley divides), head left over the tumbledown wall (markerpost) to reach a bridlegate (beside a dew pond). After the bridlegate, follow the path to the right skirting around the pond (SP 'Wolfscote Dale') heading down Biggin Dale alongside the wall on your right. Follow this path heading down along the floor of this steep-sided valley for 1.25 miles, initially sparsely wooded with scree slopes then more densely wooded (nature reserve) beyond which the path leads down passing scree slopes and scrub woodland to reach the confluence with Wolfscote Dale and the River Dove across your path.

*3.* Turn left along the clear gravel path through a squeeze-stile and follow this path heading down through Wolfscote Dale along the wooded banks of the River Dove (with the river on your right) for 1.75 miles to eventually reach the road beside a bridge across the River Dove at the hamlet of Lode Mill (just past two semi-detached cottages on your left). Turn left along the road then, after a few paces, follow the roadside path to your right (SP 'Shining Tor') which leads steadily up alongside the road then, where the road bends sharply up to the left, turn right (SP 'Tissington' and National Trust sign 'Pinch Bank'). Follow this path climbing steeply up alongside a wall on your left to reach a junction of paths at the top of the bank. Turn right (SP 'Milldale') heading along the top of the bank alongside the wall on your left, with the valley falling steeply away to your right. Just after the promontory of Shining Tor, the grassy path curves round to the left (wall still on your left and Mill Dale down to your right) to reach a wall-stile across your path. Cross the stile and head to the right down across the hillside, with the walls on either side funnelling you to reach the top of a steep bank above Milldale. A path now winds steeply down to reach Viator's Bridge across the River Dove at Milldale.

*4.* Cross the bridge and follow the lane to the right which quickly forks in the centre of Milldale where you take the lane ahead just to the left passing Polly's Cottage (shop) and 'phone box on your left, immediately after which take the narrow FP to the left up stone steps (SP 'Alstonefield'). Follow this path up through undergrowth to reach a wall-gate that leads out onto a field, after which turn left steeply up the field keeping close to the field boundary on your left through another small wall-gate (following a line of telegraph poles), then carry on climbing up then, as you reach the top of the steep bank, head to the right across the field to a stile in the top right corner. After this stile, head diagonally to the left across the middle of the field to another stile in the far opposite corner, after which turn right up across the middle of the field to reach a gate that leads onto a road on the edge of Alstonefield. Turn left along the road into Alstonefield. As you reach the village green and The George on your left, carry straight on passing a smaller green to reach a road junction.

Turn left towards 'Hulme End, Hartington' and follow the road curving to the right passing the parking area/toilets on your left. Follow this road straight on out of Alstonefield.

5. After the last of the houses on the edge of Alstonefield, carry straight on along the road for 300 yards then, where the road bends to the left, take the FP to the right over a stile (SP). Head to the left across the field to soon join a grassy track which you follow through a gateway in a wall, after which bear right diagonally across the field to reach a small gate tucked away in the top right corner beside the small wood. After this gate, head to the left across the field to reach a wall-gate that leads onto a walled track (SP 'Beresford Dale'). Turn right along the track, bearing left at the fork in the track after a short distance and down to reach a stile beside a metal gate at the end of the walled track. After the gate, carry straight on along the track for a few paces (with a wall on your right) to quickly reach another metal gate where you turn left (before the gate) along a grassy track that leads down alongside a wall on your right into Narrowdale. Where the wall on your right bends away, carry straight on across the field to reach the end of a wall (protruding into the middle of the field) which you follow (wall on your left) to reach a stile beside a gate across your path. Cross the stile and follow the path straight on with the wall on your left through a metal bridlegate then down through Narrowdale to reach a gate at the foot of this narrow valley that leads onto a junction of tracks. Turn right along the level track alongside the wall on your left (ignore track up to right) and follow this stony track gently dropping down through a series of gates for 0.75 miles to reach a road opposite the entrance gates to Beresford House.

6. Turn right along the road to soon reach a ford/FB across the River Dove - take the FP to the left before the river and follow this riverside path up through wooded Beresford Dale with the Dove on your right. After a while a FB leads across to the other bank and a path continues upstream for a while before bearing away from the river rising up through woodland to reach a squeeze-stile at the edge of the woods (open fields ahead). Head straight on along the clear path gently rising up skirting across the flanks of Pennilow Hill then,

as you reach the end of the hill, follow the clearly marked path bearing left down across the field to reach a gate in a wall (SP). After the gate, bear right up across the field and through a gap in the wall half way up the field (SP) after which continue up the hillside across the middle of the field to pick up a clear path at the foot of a grassy bank (waymarkers) which you follow to the left up to reach a walled track. At the track, take the FP opposite and follow this straight on passing a farmhouse on your left after which drop down to the left through a metal gate that leads onto the main road through Hartington. Turn right back into the village centre.

*Hartington*

# Hartington Walking Weekend
## - Sunday Walk -
### Hartington, Dove Valley, Pilsbury Castle, the Salt Way & Sheen

| | |
|---|---|
| Highlights | The Dove Valley, Norman castles, an old salt road, the distinctive profile of Sheen Hill and a windswept village. |
| Distance | 6.5 miles       Time       3 hours |
| Maps | OS Explorer OL24 |
| Refreshments | Pubs, shops and cafés at Hartington. Pub at Sheen. |
| Terrain | From Hartington, field paths lead up through the Dove Valley across fields and rough pastures (numerous wall stiles) to reach Pilsbury Castle. From Pilsbury, a track leads down to a ford across the River Dove from where a rough track climbs up to join a road below Sheen Hill. After some road walking, a path cuts off skirting around Sheen Hill down to reach Sheen. A farm track and then field paths lead down to a footbridge across the Dove from where it is a short walk back to Hartington. |
| Ascents | Carder Low - 330 metres above sea level<br>Sheen Hill - 324 metres above sea level |
| Caution | Take care when walking along country lanes. Keep to the path across the flanks of Carder Low as there are old mine workings. |

To the north of Hartington lies the upper Dove Valley, a wonderful world of quiet paths and rolling hills criss-crossed by drystone walls. In particular, the views from the flanks of Carder Low, with its lines of bell p'ts tracing the lead ore veins underground, are superb with glimpses of the serrated ridges of Chrome Hill and Parkhouse Hill further up the valley. Suddenly, the earthworks of Pilsbury Castle come into view situated on a small limestone reef knoll overlooking the valley. The earthworks of this Norman motte and bailey castle are clearly visible with its high central mound, originally crowned by a wooden watchtower around which would have been two baileys where timber stables, kitchens and accommodation buildings once stood surrounded by a ditch and wooden palisade. This castle dates from the late 11th Century, built after the unsuccessful rebellion by the Northern barons against William I who then carried out his terrible 'Harrying of the North' in retribution; castles such as this sprang up across the North as a show of Norman strength. The vast Manor of Hartington had been given to Henry De Ferrers, loyal knight of William I, who controlled it from this castle. It was only used for a few decades before being abandoned in favour of nearby Hartington that had begun to grow as a trading centre.

From Pilsbury, an old track leads down to a ford across the River Dove before climbing up to join a lane in the shadow of Sheen Hill, passing the 16th Century Broadmeadow Hall along the way, once the home of the Sleigh family. This track is an old packhorse and salt road that linked Cheshire with Chesterfield; salt was a valuable commodity centuries ago, used to cure food. Just to the south of Sheen Hill, with its distinctive summit capped by a prominent outcrop, lies the windswept village of Sheen, a scattered farming community situated on a broad ridge of land between the Dove and Manifold valleys. Sheen Church, dedicated to St Luke, was rebuilt in Victorian times although it stands on the site of a 12th Century chapel that belonged to Burton Abbey. The church tower is a well-known landmark visible for miles around.

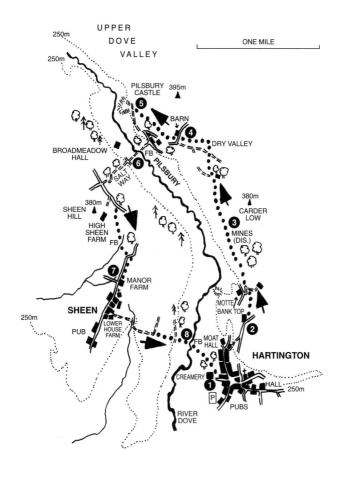

# THE WALK

1. From the market square in the centre of Hartington (with your back to the Devonshire Arms) head straight on along the road across the square (road-sign 'Pilsbury') passing the pond on your left. Follow this road straight on heading out of Hartington then, just after the road bends to the right at the entrance to Moat Hall (road-signs 'gates' & 'cattle grid'), take the rutted concrete track up to the right immediately before the last house on your right on the edge of the village. Follow this track climbing up to soon reach the driveway to a cottage where you carry straight on along the enclosed grassy track climbing above the cottage up to reach a road. Turn left along the road and follow this up passing a farmhouse on your left just after which take the FP to the left over a wall-stile immediately after the barn (SP).

2. After the stile, bear very slightly to the right across the field to quickly reach another wall-stile (markerpost), after which bear left across the field over another stile then straight on across the next field (heading towards the farm buildings ahead) to reach a wall-stile. Cross this stile and turn left alongside the wall on your left (do not head up towards farm buildings) to join a farm track at a gate. Turn left through a wall-gate immediately before this gate then right to re-join the farm track just beyond the gate (quirky section of path!). Follow this track downhill then, where this track bends sharply down to the left after a short distance, head right through a gate on this bend (waymarker). After the gate, head straight on bearing slightly up to the right to join the wall on your right, which you follow straight on along the top of a bank. Where this wall turns away (way-marker), carry straight on bearing slightly to the left across the hillside along an indistinct grassy path. Follow this path straight on across the middle of the gently sloping hillside heading up the valley, keeping to roughly the same contour (occasional markerposts), to reach a large gap in the corner of a tumbledown wall. After this wall gap, carry straight on bearing very slightly to the right to reach a wall-stile, after which continue straight on passing a line of old mine

workings to reach another wall-stile that leads out onto the rough grassy flanks of Carder Low.

3. Follow the broad grassy path straight on across the 'shoulder' of Carder Low to soon reach a small wall-gate, after which bear right up across the middle of the field and through a large gap in the wall three-quarters of the way up the field. After the wall gap, head straight across the next field through a small wall-gate beside a gate (immediately to the left of the copse of trees). After the wall-gate, follow the path bearing to the right straight on (ignore track down to left) up across low limestone outcrops to join a wall corner just above the outcrops (SP). Carry straight on bearing to the right up across the rough field, passing to the left of another wall corner and then straight on over a track to reach a wall-stile (waymarker). Cross the wall-stile and drop down the hillside alongside the wall on your right into the bottom of a dry valley where you turn left (SP 'Pilsbury & Crowdecote') down along the bottom of the valley to join a road beside a large barn.

4. At the road, take the FP opposite (SP 'Crowdecote') and walk across the field bearing very slightly to the left and over a wall-stile then straight on over another wall-stile. After this second wall-stile, carry straight on alongside the wall on your right heading up the valley and over a wall across your path after 0.25 miles *(view ahead of upper Dove Valley)*. After this wall, drop down the hillside alongside the wall on your right (Pilsbury Castle comes into view) to reach a grassy track and wall across your path with Pilsbury Castle in front of you. *Access to Pilsbury Castle via the small gate in the wall.*

5. Turn left along the grassy track (with the wall on your right) heading back down through the Dove Valley and follow this track for 0.25 miles to reach the road on a sharp bend on the edge of the hamlet of Pilsbury. *(NB: The grassy track from Pilsbury Castle to the hamlet of Pilsbury is a concessionary path. If this is no longer available, re-trace your steps back from Pilsbury Castle to reach the road beside the large barn, where you turn right down into Pilsbury).* At the road (on the sharp bend), turn right into Pilsbury passing below a large three-storey

house on your left and through a gate across the road, after which turn right down along a stony track (SP 'Sheen, Brund') to reach a ford/FB across the River Dove.

6. After the ford, follow the track climbing up the hillside to soon reach a 'crossroads' of tracks where you carry straight on along the enclosed grassy track (SP 'Brund') climbing steadily alongside a wall on your left all the way up (keep to enclosed track) to reach a road at the top of the climb. Turn left along the road for 0.25 miles with Sheen Hill across to your right then, as the road curves to the left, take the FP to the right through a squeeze-stile (SP). Walk straight across the field alongside fence/hedge on your right to reach a squeeze-stile in the field corner (boggy ground), after which head diagonally to the left across the middle of the field to reach another squeeze-stile in the far opposite corner. After this squeeze-stile, walk straight on across the middle of the field (passing to the left of some hawthorn trees) down to reach a stile over a fence/wall that leads over a small FB across an overgrown stream. After the FB, head to the right alongside the stream to soon reach a stile in the bottom corner of the field, after which head left up across the middle of the field to reach a stile over a fence that leads through undergrowth to join a road. Turn left along the road for a short distance then, where the road bends to the left, turn right over a stile beside a gate (SP). After the stile, head to the right down across the field alongside the hedge on your right to reach Manor Farm. As you reach the farm buildings, cross the stile to your right that leads onto the road at the top end of Sheen (SP).

7. Turn left along the road and follow it through Sheen passing St Luke's Church on your left and then Peakstones Farm after which turn left along the driveway into the farmyard of Lower House Farm (SP 'bridleway') - *pub short detour ahead*. Walk straight on through the farmyard passing between the barns to reach a double metal gate at the far end, after which follow the concrete track ahead. Follow this track gradually dropping down the hillside into the bottom of a shallow valley where you follow the track bending to the right through a gate then steadily rising up keeping close to the field edge

on your right to reach two gates in the top right corner of the field (where the track bends sharp left). Head straight on through the left-hand gate (do not continue along concrete track) and walk straight across the field to reach a bridle-gate in a wall, after which follow the path ahead down through a 'cleft' heading down the hillside *(Hartington comes into view)* to reach a track across your path. At the track, take the FP opposite through a small gate beside a field gate (SP 'Hartington') and walk straight across the field to reach a FB across the River Dove.

8. After the FB, follow the path to the right that leads through a large gap in the overgrown hedge in the field corner, after which carry straight on to reach a squeeze-stile to the left of a wall corner. After the squeeze-stile, bear left slightly across the field and through two wall-stiles (markerposts) then straight across a large field to reach a small gate in the far left corner that leads into woodland. Walk through this belt of woodland and through another small gate, after which head straight across the field to join a road beside the entrance to the former cheese factory. Turn left back into Hartington.

# HATHERSAGE

*Hathersage is a bustling village set on the slopes of the Derwent Valley with the jagged crest of Stanage Edge dominating the skyline. First settled in Saxon times, the village developed on the rise of land known as Bank Top where the Parish Church now stands, indeed, beside the church are earthworks known as Camp Green that date back to the Dark Ages. The Church of St Michael and All Angels was first mentioned in the early 12th Century, although the present church was built in the 14th Century with some 15th Century additions by Sir Robert Eyre, who fought with Henry V at Agincourt and restored the church upon his safe return. The church is noted for its collection of 15th Century memorial brasses of Sir Robert Eyre and his family. Hathersage is famed as the last resting place of Little John, "friend and lieutenant of Robin Hood" and one-time resident of Hathersage whose grave can be found in the churchyard. In medieval times, Hathersage stood on the edge of Sherwood Forest and nearby Loxley is said to be the birthplace of Robin Hood. Indeed, there are several places locally that bear his name including Hood Brook and Robin Hood's Cave - this whole area was once the stomping ground of England's famed outlaw! Hathersage remained a small agricultural village up until the 18th Century when mills and quarries began to open, attracted by the abundant supply of water power and quality grindstones hewn from the surrounding gritstone edges. Hathersage was once a major centre for brass button, needle and wire making and home to England's first needle-making factory in the 1560's. The industry flourished during the 19th Century with five needle mills throughout the village, although working conditions were horrendous. By the turn of the 20th Century, the businesses had moved to Sheffield.*

## THE VILLAGE

Hathersage boasts five pubs, a Youth Hostel, B&B's, café, restaurant, delicatessen, general stores, outdoor pursuit shops, Post Office, chemist, doctor's surgery, NatWest bank, Royal Bank of Scotland, outdoor swimming pool, toilets, car park, garage, bus service and railway station (Hope Valley Line).

## ACCOMMODATION

Castleton Information Centre:        01433 620679

## HATHERSAGE PUBS

**The Scotsmans Pack, Hathersage:**      **01433 650253**
This lovely pub is set in the historic heart of Hathersage. It has a traditional atmosphere with a cosy corner around an attractive fireplace. The pub stands at the foot of the steep tracks that climb up across the moors, once busy with packhorses as well as travelling tradesmen from Scotland who sold their wares to local farmers.

**The George Hotel, Hathersage:**      **01433 650436**
There has been an inn on this site since at least the 15th Century, originally an alehouse serving the 'jaggers' along the packhorse trails between Castleton and Sheffield. It later became a coaching inn and is now a plush hotel with a large dining room and comfortable bar.

**The Little John Inn, Hathersage:**      **01433 650225**
Traditional Victorian pub in the centre of Hathersage with several rooms including a dining room, bar and games room. Note the original stained glass windows.

**Millstone Inn, Hathersage Booths:**      **01433 650258**
This large pub is situated high on the hillside below Millstone Edge overlooking the valley, a mile outside Hathersage along the main road to Sheffield (bus stop outside the pub!). There are wonderful views from the large, comfortable lounge and adjoining Terrace restaurant.

**The Plough Inn, Leadmill Bridge:**        **01433 650319**

Just over half a mile out of Hathersage, this comfortable pub is renowned for the quality of its food. Inside, the bar is cosy with log fires, pewter tankards hanging from the low beams and well-kept beer. There is also a split-level eating area and separate dining room whilst outside is an enclosed courtyard.

## PUBS ON THE WALKS

Barrel Inn, Bretton:                    01433 630856

*Hathersage*

# Hathersage Walking Weekend
## - Saturday Walk -
### *Hathersage, Bretton Clough, Barrel Inn, Abney Moor & the River Derwent*

## WALK INFORMATION

| | |
|---|---|
| Highlights | Two manor houses of the Eyre family, wooded cloughs, Derbyshire's highest pub, wonderful moorland, incredible views and walking alongside the Derwent. |
| Distance | 11 miles      Time      5 hours |
| Maps | OS Explorer OL1 and OL24 |
| Refreshments | Pubs, shops and cafés at Hathersage. Pubs at Leadmill and Bretton. |
| Terrain | Field paths and quiet lanes lead up to Highlow Hall, from where a path drops steeply down into the wooded confines of Highlow Brook. A muddy path leads up through this valley to reach Stoke Ford then heads up through Bretton Clough (boggy in places) before a steep climb through woodland to Bretton. After some road walking, a path drops steeply down into the upper reaches of Bretton Clough then climbs to reach Abney Grange. A path then heads across Abney Moor to join the stony track of Shatton Lane, which skirts across Shatton Moor before a rough path heads across Offerton Moor to reach Offerton Hall. A grassy path leads down to join the banks of the River Derwent from where a riverside path returns to Leadmill Bridge. |
| Ascents: | Abney Moor - 390 metres above sea level. |
| Caution: | Several steep sections in particular the descent into Bretton Clough from Hucklow Edge. The path up through Highlow Brook and Bretton Clough is muddy. |

# POINTS OF INTEREST

The imposing 16th Century manor house of Highlow Hall overlooks the wooded ravine of Highlow Brook with the heather-clad Eyam Moor stretching away to the south. The rather amusing name of this fortified farmhouse actually means 'high hill' as 'low' comes from the Old English word meaning 'hill'. This was once the home of Robert Eyre, head of the influential Eyre family who held a score of manors throughout this area. It is said that he built a manor house for each his seven sons within sight of Highlow Hall - our route passes Offerton Hall later on this walk. From here, a path leads down into the wooded confines of Highlow Brook to reach an old ford across the stream then heads up through this delightful valley to reach Stoke Ford at the confluence of Abney Clough and Bretton Clough where five old packhorse routes converge. Of the many deep wooded valleys that dissect Eyam Moor and Abney Moor, Bretton Clough is the most impressive; secluded, beautiful and wild with ancient woodland cloaking its steep sides. This whole area is like a huge island of hills and valleys with steep escarpments falling away on all sides. Often overlooked by visitors to the Peak District, this is walking country par excellence!

Abney Grange is situated above the dramatic upper reaches of Bretton Clough; in medieval times, this was the site of a monastic farm that belonged to Rufford Abbey as the suffix 'grange' indicates. To the north of this hamlet lies Abney Moor, an expansive swathe of moorland that sweeps down towards Abney Clough with far-reaching views across rolling hills and valleys. At its northern edge our route joins an old road known as Shatton Lane, now just a rough track, which skirts around the upper flanks of Shatton Moor high above the Hope Valley. The views are amongst the finest in the Peak District with Castleton, Mam Tor and Win Hill laid out before you. The track curves round into the Derwent Valley passing a conspicuous radio mast, then Hathersage comes into view with Higger Tor, Carl Wark and Millstone Edge rising above.

*For more information about Bretton Clough & the Barrel Inn, see Walking Weekend 5*

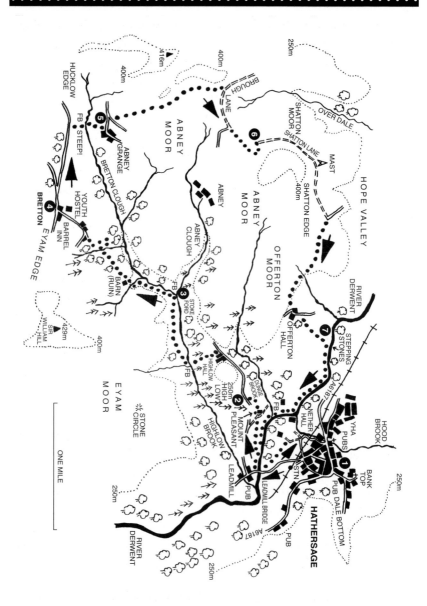

# THE WALK

*1.* Leave Hathersage along the road-turning opposite the George Hotel (B6001) towards 'Grindleford, Bakewell' and follow this out of the village, down beneath the railway bridge and continue on to reach Leadmill Bridge across the River Derwent. Take the FP to the right immediately after the bridge (SP 'Shatton') and follow the riverside path straight on for about 200 yards then, just after a dilapidated barn near a weir along the river, head left alongside an old fence-line away from the river then up a short but steep wooded bank to reach a stile beside a gate at the top of the bank. After the stile, turn right along the top of the wooded bank gently rising up alongside the fence/wall on your right then, where this woodland ends and the wall turns downhill, carry straight on along the grassy track up to reach a gate that leads onto a junction of lanes just below Mount Pleasant Farm. Head straight on up along the left-hand lane ahead (to the left of the entrance lane to Mount Pleasant Farm) and follow this up through the farmyard (farmhouse to your right) to reach a stile beside a gate that leads out onto a field *(a permissive path skirts to the left around this farmyard)*. Head straight on bearing slightly to the left to join a wall/wooded bank on your left which you follow round to reach a bridlegate across your path, after which follow the grassy path straight on bearing slightly to the left up across the field to reach a stile over a small section of wall that leads onto a road.

*2.* Turn right up along the road and follow it to reach Highlow Hall. Continue along the road passing the farm buildings and entrance to the Hall then, after about 50 yards, take the FP to the left through a double metal gate that leads into the field (immediately after the two-storey ornate stone barn). After the gate, follow the rough track straight down alongside the wall on your left passing the ornate barn (Hall across to your left) then, where the wall on your left ends (old stone gatepost) just after you have passed the Hall, bear off to the right down the hillside alongside a line of trees down to reach a gate in the wall at the bottom of the field. Head through the gate and follow the track quite steeply down through Highlow Wood to reach a ford/FB across Highlow Brook. Cross the stream and follow the clear track climbing up with the small side-stream on your left at first then bending up to the right through woodland. Follow this stony track rising up across the wooded hillside to reach a gate at the top of the wooded bank, after which continue along the track rising up across the hillside keeping close to the fence on your right (Highlow Brook down to your right) then, where the track levels out slightly and forks, follow the grassy path to the right alongside the fence on your right (waymarker post) leaving the clearer track to climb up the hillside. Follow this undulating path straight on across the hillside heading up the valley then traversing a small side-valley, after which continue straight on along the path through woodland to reach the FB at Stoke Ford *(confluence of Bretton Clough and Abney Clough)*.

3. Do not cross the FB but take the FP up to the left (SP 'Public Footpath by Gotherage Barn to Grindleford and to Eyam') through woodland then, where the path forks after a short distance, follow the right-hand path straight on heading across the steep wooded hillside (Bretton Brook down to your right) through gorse and trees to reach a stile in a wall. Cross the stile and continue straight on across the wooded hillside then follow the path as it curves round into a wooded side-valley to reach an old bridge across a small stream. Cross the bridge and follow the path straight on up a grassy bank passing below the ruins of Gotherage Barn. The path levels out and leads straight on across undulating fields crossing tumbledown walls before skirting the foot of a wooded bank (boggy ground) beyond which the path gently rises up to reach a fence and wooded ravine across your path. Follow the path to the left (alongside the ravine) up to reach a stile to the right that leads over the small stream. After the stream, follow the path ahead bending sharp left after a short distance climbing up across the steep wooded hillside (ravine to your left) before zig-zagging steeply up to reach a stile beside a gate (above the wooded ravine). Head over the stile and follow the enclosed path straight on to reach a road beside the houses at Nether Bretton where you turn right gently rising up to reach a T-junction beside the Barrel Inn.

4. Turn right along the road heading along the top of Eyam Edge then, where the road forks after 250 yards, take the turning to the right heading straight on along the top of Hucklow Edge. Follow this road along the top of the Edge for just over 0.5 miles then, about 100 yards before the road bends to the left down from the Edge, take the FP to the right over a wall-stile (SP). Follow the path alongside the wall on your right steeply down into Bretton Clough to reach a FB across the stream in the valley bottom. Cross the FB and follow the path to the right climbing steeply up the hillside to join a wall on your right which you follow steeply up out of the confines of the clough then more steadily up across the field (wall still on your right) then, as you near the top corner of this field, cross the wall-stile to your right (Abney Grange just ahead). After the stile, walk straight on keeping close to the wall on your right passing the farm buildings to reach a wall-stile in the field corner (near the barns) that leads onto the road just above the hamlet of Abney Grange.

5. Turn left up along the road to soon reach a junction with another road where you turn right back on yourself slightly and follow this road for 50 yards then turn left over a stile beside a gate (SP) - *Abney Grange just down to your right*. Follow the wide grassy path straight on for 1 mile across Abney Moor, gently rising up at first *(Win Hill comes into view ahead at the highest point)* then straight on along an undulating path across open moorland to join the walled track of Brough Lane across your path. Turn right along this track and follow it gently curving round to soon reach a crossroads of tracks (top of a metalled lane on your right). Carry straight on along the track (SP 'Shatton') gradually heading up alongside the wall on your right. As you reach the foot of the 'summit' shoulder of Shatton Moor (track levels out), follow the track bending round to the left (away from the wall) for a short distance then bending sharp right through a gate at the top of the walled track of Shatton Lane (SP).

6. Follow this walled track straight on following the curve of the hillside round passing the radio mast beneath Shatton Edge, after which the track gradually drops down then, where the track becomes a metalled lane and bends sharply down to the left, head to the right

through a bridlegate in a wall on this bend (SP). After the gate, head straight on along the rough track bearing slightly to the right across the hillside to reach the top of a wall corner. Follow the undulating path straight on alongside this wall on your left for 0.75 miles heading across the flanks of Offerton Moor to reach a road just before Offerton Hall. Turn left down along the road passing between Offerton Hall and Offerton House then, immediately after the houses, take the FP to the right through a gate. Follow the enclosed path down to a gate, after which head along the grassy path down across the hillside through two gates to reach the River Derwent by the stepping stones.

7. Do not cross the stepping stones but turn right and follow the riverside path (river on your left) alongside the Derwent for 1.25 miles to reach Leadmill Bridge. Turn left over the bridge, immediately after which take the FP to the left through a squeeze-stile (SP) and follow the path straight on alongside the fence on your left heading across the field. The path becomes a clearer gravel path after a while which you follow up (fence still on your left) to join a farm track. Follow this track straight on to join a road beside the entrance to Nether Hall. Head left along the road and follow it bending to the right beneath the railway viaduct then straight on up along Mill Lane back into Hathersage.

# Hathersage Walking Weekend
## - Sunday Walk -
### *Hathersage, North Lees, Stanage Edge, Higger Tor & Carl Wark*

## WALK INFORMATION

| | |
|---|---|
| Highlights | Jane Eyre and Mr Rochester, Roman Roads and packhorse trails, a wonderful walk along Peakland's finest Edge, an outlaw's hideout and an Iron Age hill-fort. |

| | | | |
|---|---|---|---|
| Distance | 7 miles | Time | 3 hours |

| | |
|---|---|
| Maps | OS Explorer OL1 |
| Refreshments | Pubs, shops & cafés at Hathersage. No facilities en route. |
| Terrain | Field paths and tracks lead up through Hood Brook valley, with a climb up passing North Lees Hall to join the road below Stanage Edge. A rough path climbs steadily up through woodland and across boulders up onto Stanage Edge. A path follows the top of the Edge (exposed) all the way to reach its southern end, from where a moorland path leads on to join the road near Upper Burbage Bridge. Moorland paths then skirt above Burbage Brook with a sharp climb to and from Higger Tor. A path then heads across moorland to join a road from where field paths and tracks lead back to Hathersage. |
| Ascents | Stanage Edge - 457 metres above sea level. |
| Caution | This walk includes several steep sections in particular the climb to and from Stanage Edge and Higger Tor (some scrambling over boulders). Keep away from the edge of Stanage Edge - sheer drops and hidden crevices. |
| Open Access | The path along Stanage Edge heads across Open Access land. See local signs or www.openaccess.gov.uk |

# POINTS OF INTEREST

North Lees Hall is a fine tower house with a commanding position overlooking the valley. Built in the 1590's by William Jessop, it was later occupied by the Eyre family between 1750 and 1882 and is now owned by the National Park Authority. It is most famous for its associations with Charlotte Brontë, who stayed at Hathersage vicarage in 1845 and based many of the places and people in her novel Jane Eyre on her experiences during her stay. She used North Lees Hall as the basis for Mr Rochester's Thornfield Hall and also borrowed the surname of the landlord of the George Hotel when she renamed Hathersage as Morton.

The old packhorse route between Cheshire and Sheffield climbs up through Stanage Plantation onto the crest of Stanage Edge. This trod then joins the old track known as the Long Causeway, which itself follows the line of a Roman road that heads across the moors passing Stanage Pole, used for centuries as a border marker and guidepost; Stanage Edge still marks the boundary between Yorkshire and Derbyshire. Stanage Edge is the longest and most dramatic of Peakland's eastern edges, a huge escarpment of jagged rocks that rises up from a sea of heather like the crest of a mighty wave. The views are extensive with hills rising and falling as far as the eye can see. Look out for a path that leads down to a platform just below the edge with hollows and precarious edges - the farthest hollow is known as Robin Hood's Cave and was possibly one of his hide-outs. Rock climbing began here in the 1890's and Stanage Edge is now one of the most famous gritstone edges in the country with hundreds of mapped routes.

Higger Tor rises up above the delightful moorland valley of Burbage Brook, a flat-topped natural tor of resistant gritstone rock fringed by outcrops and a prominent landmark for miles around. Just to the south is the smaller tor of Carl Wark, a naturally defensive site that was used from the Iron Age through to the Dark Ages as a hill-fort. This plateau is surrounded on three sides by boulder-strewn slopes that fall steeply away towards Burbage Brook whilst a wall rampart was built to defend its western side. Carl Wark is one of the finest prehistoric defensive sites in the Peak District.

# HATHERSAGE SUNDAY WALK

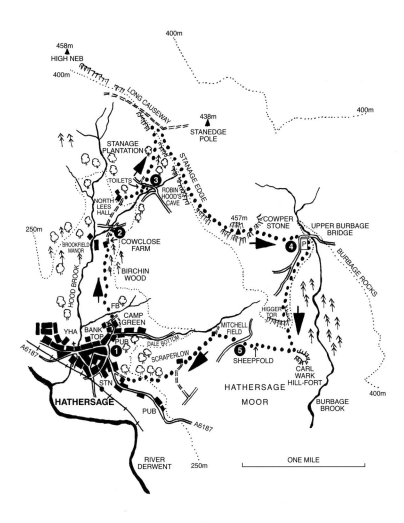

# THE WALK

1. From the centre of Hathersage, walk up along the main road through the village towards Sheffield then, where the road curves round to the right at the top of the village, turn left along School Lane. Follow this road straight on then, as you reach the Scotsmans Pack, turn left along Church Bank climbing steeply up to reach the entrance gates to the Church. Continue straight on along the lane then, where it bends sharp left around the churchyard, head straight on over a stile beside a gate (on this bend). Follow the wide grassy track to the right then, after 50 yards, take the FP to the left (waymarker post) steeply down the hillside (steps) to reach a slab FB across a stream. Cross the FB and walk straight on alongside the hedge on your left heading up the field then, as the field levels out (waymarker post), bear right up to reach a clear path at the top of the field that leads through undergrowth to quickly reach a stile. Cross the stile and head straight on alongside the field boundary/trees on your left all the way to reach Cowclose Farm. As you reach the farm, head through the gate then follow the path to the right skirting around the buildings to reach a small gate, after which head straight on across the grassy hillside (walking parallel with the farm track just to your left). As you reach the brow of a steep wooded bank above the track (and Hood Brook), follow the path bearing to the right across the wooded hillside to reach a stile that leads onto the road.

2. Turn left along the road passing North Lees Campsite (and the track towards Cowclose Farm on your left), a short distance after which turn right along a lane (SP) up to reach North Lees Hall. As you reach the hall, head straight on along the walled track and follow it bending round to the left above the hall to soon reach a 'junction' with a rough track to your right beside a stone waymarker post and information board. Turn right along this track back on yourself slightly and through a gate, after which follow the grassy track bearing slightly to the right up across the field and through a gate that leads into woodland. Follow the track up through the woods (ravine down to your right) then, as you approach the top of the

woods, a path branches up to the left (stone steps) to join the road beside a toilet block (Stanage Edge ahead).

3. Turn left along the road for 25 yards then take the BW to the right (SP) along a wide grassy path and follow this up across rough ground to soon join a clearer path which you follow up to reach a gate on the edge of Stanage Plantation. A paved trod now bears left up through the woods to reach another gate at the top of the woods, after which a stone-paved path climbs up across the boulder-strewn hillside onto the crest of Stanage Edge. Turn right and follow the path along the top of the Edge (boggy and rocky in places) - the path is level for the first 0.75 miles (keep to the path along the top of the escarpment) then gradually rises up for a further 0.5 miles to reach a Trig Point on top of a large group of outcrops at the southern end of Stanage Edge. As you reach the Trig Point, turn left across the outcrops to quickly pick up a clear path (stone-flagged in places) and follow this down across the boulder-strewn moorland then, as you reach the edge of the outcrops (large Cowper Stone just ahead), the path turns down to the right across boulders (easy scrambling). A clear moorland path now leads straight on to join the road near Upper Burbage Bridge.

4. Head left along the road and turn right into the parking area just before Upper Burbage Bridge then almost immediately take the FP to the left through the small gate (SP). After the gate, follow the path to the right heading up across the moorland, with Burbage Brook valley falling away to your left. The path levels out after a while and leads on to reach the foot of Higger Tor where a clear path (steps) leads steeply up onto its 'summit' plateau. As you reach the flat 'summit', head left at the junction of paths and follow the wide eroded path, keeping close to the edge on your left, to reach the south-eastern (bottom left) edge of Higger Tor and a small promontory of outcrops. Follow the path down across the outcrops (easy scrambling) to pick up a clear stone-pitched path that leads straight on down across moorland towards the distinctive 'tor' of Carl Wark (Iron Age hill-fort). Just before you reach the foot of the steep bank of Carl Wark (about 10 yards before the 'crossroads' of grassy paths at the foot of this bank) turn right back on yourself slightly

along a narrow grassy path heading across open moorland. Follow this path straight on (Higger Tor across to your right) to reach the right-hand side of a rectangular stone livestock enclosure. As you reach the enclosure, carry straight on (enclosure on your left) then, where the enclosure ends, follow the grassy path bearing to the right (ignore wide path off to the left after a short distance) heading straight on down to join a wall on your left which you follow down to quickly reach a small gate that leads onto a road.

5. At the road, cross the stile opposite and follow the grassy path to the left slanting down across the hillside to reach Mitchell Field Farm. As you reach the farm buildings, turn left along the stony track (SP) to quickly reach the farm entrance where you head left again for a few paces then take the FP to the right (SP) up to reach a wall-stile. Cross the wall-stile and bear right up over another wall-stile, after which head left up across the middle of the rough field along an indistinct grassy path to reach a gate in a wall that leads onto the driveway of Scraperlow House. Turn left along the driveway and through the entrance gate, after which continue along the track for a short distance then, where the track bends left, carry straight on across the field alongside the wall on your right to reach a stile that leads down onto a clear path beside a gate. Do not head through the gate, but drop down to the left over a stile that leads onto an enclosed sunken path through woodland. Follow this sunken path down through woodland then, as you approach the bottom of the woods, follow the path down to the left to reach a gate at the top of an enclosed path. Follow this enclosed path down to join a lane beside a house that leads down to reach the road at the top end of Hathersage *(caution – this lane emerges onto a busy road)*. Turn right along this road back into Hathersage.

# HAYFIELD

*Hayfield is a delightful mix of Pennine mill town and Peakland village, an outpost of Derbyshire that looks towards Stockport and Manchester. The reason for this contrasting character is its geography for it lies cradled amongst the hills of the Upper Sett Valley on the north-western edge of the Peak District National Park with the dramatic escarpment of Kinder Scout tracing across the skyline just to the east forming a physical barrier between Hayfield and the rest of Derbyshire. In Roman times, the road between Buxton and the fort at Glossop came through Hayfield, although the village itself is probably of Saxon origins and was first mentioned in the Domesday Book when it was little more than a forest clearing. Following the Conquest, this small settlement found itself within the boundary of the Royal Forest of the Peak, a Norman hunting preserve administered from Peveril Castle at Castleton. It remained a small farming community for many centuries, although the forest was gradually encroached upon. Things changed dramatically in the 18th Century as demand for woven woollen cloth grew from the burgeoning towns of Stockport and Manchester. This heralded a period of prosperity as a thriving cottage industry developed and houses were rebuilt as three-storey weavers' cottages with handlooms in the light and airy upper floors. By the early 19th Century, water-powered mills began to take over with several built alongside the River Sett and its tributaries where cotton, rather than wool, was spun. Other industries also sprang up including calico printing, paper mills and quarries. The railway arrived in 1868 linking Hayfield with Manchester, bringing goods to and from the mills and thousands of walkers at weekends during its heyday in the 1920's and 30's. The mills and railway are now closed and Hayfield has returned to a quiet rural village and popular walking base.*

## THE VILLAGE

Hayfield offers six pubs, B&B's, campsite, restaurants, fish & chip shop, butcher's shop, cafés, general stores, off licence, chemist, Post Office, newsagent, hairdresser's shop, art gallery, Hayfield Countryside Centre (Tourist Information), bus service, car park and toilets.

## ACCOMMODATION

Tourist Information Centre, Glossop:    01457 855920
Hayfield Countryside Centre:    01663 746222

## HAYFIELD PUBS

### Bull's Head, Hayfield:    01663 745511

Situated beside the church in the centre of Hayfield, this 18th Century three-storey pub is a traditional locals' pub with low beams and an open fire in the front bar and a games room to the rear. No accommodation

### George Hotel, Hayfield:    01663 743691

Dating back to 1575, this old pub was a Posting House in the 19th Century. Inside, there is a small, cosy bar and snug with low ceilings as well as a separate dining room and lounge with a lovely old cast-iron range.

### Kinder Lodge, Hayfield:    01663 743613

Situated on New Mills Road just outside the village centre, this old 18th Century weavers' cottage is now a lively locals' pub that has an emphasis on sport with big screen TV, pool table and a good selection of Real Ales.

### Packhorse, Hayfield:    01663 740074

This historic pub stands at the start of the packhorse trail over the hills to Edale. There has been a pub on this site for many centuries, although the present building is Victorian. It has a traditional yet contemporary feel with a bright, modern interior as well as wood panelling and comfy sofas. No accommodation.

**Royal Hotel, Hayfield :**         **01663 742721**

Situated next to the village cricket ground and overlooking the River Sett, this three-story Georgian building was originally the vicarage, although it has been known as the Royal Hotel since the 1860's. Inside, several wood-panelled rooms are served by a central bar with open fires and high ceilings.

**Sportsman Inn, Kinder Road, Hayfield:**    **01663 741565**

This traditional pub is situated just outside Hayfield in the Sett Valley along the busy route up to Kinder Scout (and near the campsite). Inside, there are several cosy rooms including a comfortable lounge with a lovely stone fireplace and low beams.

## PUBS ALONG THE WALKS

Lantern Pike, Little Hayfield:         01663 747590

# Hayfield Walking Weekend
## - Saturday Walk -
### Hayfield, Edale Cross, Kinder Downfall & Snake Path

## WALK INFORMATION

| | |
|---|---|
| Highlights | Dramatic cloughs, packhorse trails and a wayside cross, weathered rocks, incredible views, walking across the plateau, steep escarpments, a plunging waterfall and the Mass Trespass. |
| Distance | 10.5 miles        Time       5 - 6 hours |
| Maps | OS Explorer OL1 |
| Refreshments | Pubs, cafés and shops at Hayfield. Sportsman Inn near Bowden Bridge towards the end of the walk. No other facilities en route - take plenty of provisions with you. |
| Terrain | Farm tracks lead over into the Sett Valley from where a stony track climbs up for 1.5 miles to reach Edale Cross at the top of the 'pass'. A well-trodden moorland path (flagstones in places) climbs up passing Edale Rocks to reach the plateau at Kinder Low. A clear but rough path then follows this plateau edge all the way to Kinder Downfall, from where an undulating path continues along the plateau edge (rocky sections) to reach its north-western tip above the 'saddle' at Ashop Head. A pitched-stone path leads steeply down into this saddle from where a path turns down into William Clough. Steep at first, this narrow path heads down through the ravine, crossing and re-crossing the stream. From the foot of the clough, a path heads across White Brow above Kinder Reservoir then drops down to join Kinder Road which leads back into Hayfield. |

| Ascents | Kinder Low - 633 metres above sea level |
|---|---|
| Caution | This is a strenuous walk with a long climb up onto Kinder Scout. There are steep drops to the side of the path along the edge of the plateau. Take care around Kinder Downfall - sheer drops. The descent from Kinder Scout to Ashop Head is steep. The descent down through William Clough follows a narrow path and is steep and rough in places with some tricky sections over rocks. Navigation may be difficult, especially across Kinder Low; map and compass essential. |

*Hayfield*

# POINTS OF INTEREST

This is one of Peakland's classic walks, an exhilarating trek up onto the wild Kinder Scout plateau, tracing its spectacular western rim to reach the dramatic cleft of Kinder Downfall. The climb up through the Sett Valley is superb with the rugged peaked profile of Mount Famine and the more rounded South Head dominating the valley. From the isolated Coldwell Clough Farm, our route follows the old packhorse trail between Hayfield and Edale that climbs steadily up through a wonderful landscape of bulky hills and deep valleys to reach Edale Cross at the top of the pass. Hayfield was once at the hub of several important packhorse routes. Little has changed over the centuries and it is easy to imagine a weather-beaten jagger leading his train of packhorses along this old track. From Edale Cross, a path turns off skirting below Swine's Back to join the boot-worn route of the Pennine Way that leads steadily up passing the conspicuous Edale Rocks (outstanding viewpoint) onto the moonscape of Kinder Low (633m). This marks the south-western edge of the Kinder Scout plateau and is just three metres lower than the plateau's highest point some distance away to the east set amidst a vast landscape of deep groughs and featureless bog.

From Kinder Low, a wonderful walk ensues along the western rim of this plateau with the ground sweeping steeply away down towards Kinder Reservoir far below. The highlight of this walk is undoubtedly Kinder Downfall, Peakland's highest and most dramatic waterfall. This is where the infant River Kinder tumbles from the plateau in spectacular fashion, cascading 100-ft down through a ravine of shattered rocks and huge boulders. In summer, the water barely wets the rock but in winter when a westerly gale blows then it is a sight to behold with an updraft that sends a huge curtain of spray vertically in the air! Great care must be taken around this precipitous ravine. From Kinder Downfall, our route continues in the footsteps of Pennine Wayfarers along the plateau edge with wonderful views unfolding with every step. The path skirts the promontory of Sandy Heys before reaching the north-western tip of the plateau high above the 'saddle' of land at the source of the

River Ashop. From the crossroads of paths at Ashop Head, a path turns down into the dramatic ravine of William Clough, an exciting descent alongside a tumbling stream that feeds Kinder Reservoir, built in 1912 to slake the thirst of burgeoning Stockport with a capacity of 500 million gallons. During its construction a railway was built to move men and materials from Hayfield Station and a 'tin town' sprung up for the workers near Bowden Bridge, a 16th Century packhorse bridge by the confluence of the rivers Sett and Kinder.

The Bowden Bridge Quarry car park will forever hold a special place in walkers' hearts for this was where several hundred ramblers met on the 24th April 1932 before their Mass Trespass up onto Kinder Scout in protest at the lack of access to the open hills. These forbidden hills were out of bounds, the preserve of landowners and their gamekeepers. For people living and working in the industrial towns and cities of Northern England, a days' hill-walking offered fresh air, exercise and freedom away from the factories, but this basic right was denied by an elite who wanted to keep the hills for their grouse. They walked up William Clough to be met by a line of gamekeepers on Kinder Scout. Accounts vary, but a few scuffles broke out and the ramblers returned to Bowden Bridge only to be met by police who arrested several of the leaders. Five people were subsequently tried at Derby Assizes and sent to prison! Such harsh punishment brought widespread condemnation, changed public opinion and united access campaign groups; it even inspired folk singer Ewan McColl to write 'The Manchester Rambler'. This was the catalyst for change that led to the National Parks and Access to the Countryside Act 1949, which established this country's national parks, recorded and protected our rights of way and eventually secured access to open hill country.

*For more information about Kinder Scout, Edale Cross and the Pennine Way, see Walking Weekend 4*

# HAYFIELD SATURDAY WALK

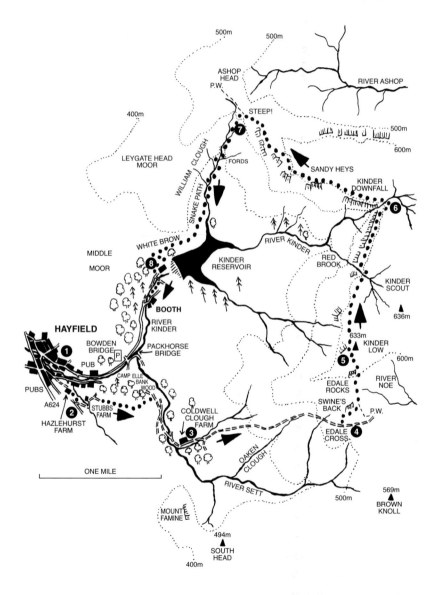

*1.* From the bridge across the River Sett in the centre of Hayfield, head up along Church Street passing St Matthew's Church on your right then, as you reach the crossroads near the top of Church Street, turn left (Old Toll House on corner) and almost immediately left again along Valley Road. Follow this road straight on then, where it bends to the left, head straight on (to the right) up along a farm lane towards Hazelhurst Farm (SP). Follow this lane gently rising up then, where the lane forks as you approach the buildings, follow the right-hand track straight on up through the farmyard of Hazelhurst Farm to reach a gate (waymarker). Head through the gate and follow the stone-flagged path bearing slightly left between the buildings (farmhouse on your right) then carry on passing behind the farmhouse, after which head up to the right along a short section of enclosed path to reach a bridlegate tucked away just beyond the farmhouse (waymarker). Head through the bridlegate and follow the enclosed grassy path gradually uphill *(Roman road)* to join a lane across your path.

*2.* Turn left along the lane (ignore entrance to Stubbs Farm to the left) and follow this stony lane straight on to reach a gate, after which follow the track curving round to the left passing above Stubbs Farm. Continue along the enclosed farm track then, where it forks 100 yards after Stubbs Farm, follow the right-hand track bending up to the right (SP) along an enclosed rough track to reach a gate at the end of the enclosed track. Head through the gate then bear left alongside a raised grassy mound (former field boundary) on your left heading up across the middle of the field passing solitary stone gateposts then, where this grassy mound bends away to the left halfway up the field, continue straight on up to reach a bridlegate in the far top corner. Head through the bridlegate and follow the path ahead, bending down to the left (enclosed by walls for much of the way) heading down across the hillside (Elle Bank Wood to your left) to reach a bridleway and bridlegate across your path on the steep hillside above the Upper Sett Valley. Turn right through the bridlegate and follow the path straight on across the steep hillside down to join a lane. Follow this lane to the right then, where it forks after a short distance, head left down to reach a bridge across the River Sett. Cross the bridge and follow the lane straight on, with the River Sett on your right, then curving round to the left up into the wooded side-valley of Coldwell Clough to reach Coldwell Clough Farm.

3. Continue along the lane passing in front of the farmhouse heading up through the side-valley, with the stream on your right, to soon reach a bridge across the stream (Coldwell Clough). Cross the bridge, after which the lane forks - follow the left-hand lane up through a gate in a wall, marked by a SP (metalled lane ends). After the gate, follow the track straight on rising steadily up alongside the wall on your left to reach a gate across the track at a crossroads of paths/tracks (wall ends on your left). Head straight on through the gate (SP 'Edale') and follow the rough track up (enclosed by fences) to reach a gate at the top of the field (National Trust sign 'Kinder Estate'). Head through the gate and follow the stony track steadily up alongside a wall on your left for a further 0.75 miles to eventually reach Edale Cross set in a small stone enclosure on your left at the top of the pass.

4. Turn left off the stony track immediately after Edale Cross through a bridlegate beside a field gate, after which head straight up the grassy hillside alongside the wall on your left for about 100 yards to reach some old stone enclosures/tumbledown wall across your path. Turn right alongside the tumbledown wall heading across the hillside below the outcrops of Swine's Back to soon join a clear path (Pennine Way). Turn left along this path passing two large stone cairns to soon reach a junction of paths beside a third large cairn set in a shallow 'dip'. Turn left along the clear path (stone-flagged for much of the way) up passing to the right side of Edale Rocks, after which a clear path leads up onto the eroded, boulder-strewn plateau of Kinder Low (OS Trig Point just across to your right).

5. Head straight on across the plateau passing between a stone-built cairn to your left and the Trig Point across to your right - continue straight on along the wide, eroded path across the plateau following a line of stone-built cairns (Kinder Reservoir comes into view) then drop down off Kinder Low across low outcrops and gritstone boulders to join the western edge of the Kinder Scout plateau, with the hillside sweeping away to your left. A clear, undulating path now leads straight on along the edge of this plateau for a further mile, gradually curving round to reach the ravine of Kinder Downfall (waterfall).

6. Cross the flat streambed of the infant River Kinder a safe distance up from the lip of the waterfall, after which follow the path to the left skirting around the rim of the rocky cleft of Kinder Downfall *(keep away from edge)*. Continue to follow this clear boulder-strewn path along the plateau edge for almost 0.5 miles to reach a stile across an old wall, after which the path rises up to reach the outcrops on the promontory of Sandy Heys. From Sandy Heys, carry straight on along the plateau edge path for a further 0.75 miles until you reach a large stone cairn at the top of a steep bank above the 'saddle' of land at Ashop Head. Follow the stone-pitched path steeply down into this 'saddle' then, as you reach the foot of the steep path (crossroads of paths just ahead), follow the stone-flagged path branching off to the left (cutting the corner off the crossroads of paths) to soon reach the clear footpath of the Snake Path.

7. Turn left along this path, which soon drops steeply down along a stone-pitched path into the narrow cleft of William Clough. A narrow path now heads down through this ravine, crossing and re-crossing the stream. After just over 0.5 miles the ravine opens out slightly and the path forks (solitary tree just ahead) - follow the right-hand path heading across the hillside. The path gradually rises up across the steep hillside to join a fence/wall on your left. Carry straight on alongside this wall (Kinder Reservoir down to your left) heading across the steep hillside for a further 0.5 miles to reach a wooden gate in the wall to your left just after an old signpost *'No dogs can be taken along this footpath unless they are held in leash'*. Turn

left through this gate and follow the track down alongside the wall on your right to reach a clear path/wall across your path (above the dam wall). Turn right and follow this path slanting down across the hillside passing above the former treatment works to join the road beside the reservoir entrance gates.

8. At the road, turn right then almost immediately left along a clear path that leads down over a bridge across the River Kinder, immediately after which turn right along a riverside path through woodland to reach a road at the hamlet of Booth. Turn right along the road, over another bridge across the river then carry on along this road (Kinder Road) heading down the valley with the river on your left to reach Bowden Quarry Car Park. Continue straight on along the road for a further 0.25 miles to reach the Sportsman Inn. As you reach the pub, turn left along a FP opposite the pub that leads down across the wooded hillside (steps) to a FB across the River Sett, after which you join a lane opposite a row of houses. Turn right along this lane and follow it heading down the valley with the river on your right all the way back into the centre of Hayfield.

# Hayfield Walking Weekend
## - Sunday Walk -
### *Hayfield, Sett Valley Trail, Lantern Pike & Little Hayfield*

## WALK INFORMATION

| | |
|---|---|
| Highlights | Full steam ahead along the Sett Valley Trail, old mills, a wonderful viewpoint, the clothier's hall and the historic Snake Path. |
| Distance | 5.5 miles          Time          2.5 hours |
| Maps | OS Explorer OL1 |
| Refreshments | Pubs and shops at Hayfield. Café at Birch Vale. Pub at Little Hayfield. |
| Terrain | This walk follows the old railway track-bed (Sett Valley Trail) between Hayfield and Birch Vale, from where a rough path and then a track climbs up out of the valley to reach Lantern Pike - the final section to the summit follows a rough, eroded path across Access Land. From Lantern Pike, field paths and old sunken paths lead down to reach the A684 at Little Hayfield. A moorland path then climbs up to join the Snake Path (superb views) which leads back down to Hayfield. |
| Ascents | Lantern Pike - 373 metres above sea level. Snake Path - 340 metres above sea level |
| Caution | The climb up to Lantern Pike is long and steady with some steep and/or rough sections. Take care crossing the A624 at Hayfield and Little Hayfield. |

# POINTS OF INTEREST

The Sett Valley Trail is a delightful wooded walkway along the track-bed of the former Hayfield to Manchester railway. This railway opened in 1868 and was, for many years, a busy line that served the numerous mills throughout the valley. It also brought thousands of walkers to Hayfield on summer Sundays during the 1930's en route to the hills. The railway closed between New Mills and Hayfield in 1970 but Derbyshire County Council purchased the track-bed and opened the Sett Valley Trail in 1979, with the old station forming a car park and information centre. The trail leads through the valley passing former mill ponds to reach Birch Vale, once home to a large calico print works; note the curving terrace of cottages known as The Crescent in Spinnerbottom. From here, an old path and then a track climbs steadily up to reach the heather-clad hill of Lantern Pike. Despite its modest height, the prospect is superb with Kinder Scout to the east, Axe Edge to the south, the Cheshire plain and Stockport's tower blocks to the west and a bird's eye view of Hayfield beneath your feet. Used as a warning beacon centuries ago, this hill is now under the care of The National Trust.

An old sunken path leads down from Lantern Pike to reach the hamlet of Little Hayfield, which is dominated by the five-storey Clough Mill that towers above the old millworkers' cottages set in a wooded clough. There has been a cotton mill on this site since the 1830's, although production ceased in the 1920's. The mill is now apartments. From Little Hayfield, a track leads up through woodland towards Park Hall, built in the 18th Century by Joseph Hague who made his money from cotton. A path then strikes across Middle Moor climbing gently up through heather to join the historic Snake Path. This path was established in 1897 by agreement between the Peak and Northern Counties Footpath Preservation Society and the Duke of Devonshire and links Hayfield with the Snake Pass road through the Woodlands Valley. The descent along the Snake Path back towards Hayfield is superb with views along the Sett Valley and Lantern Pike rising above, whilst to the south the peaks of Mount Famine and South Head dominate. Note the copse of trees known locally as Twenty Trees, although I only counted 19!

142

# HAYFIELD SUNDAY WALK

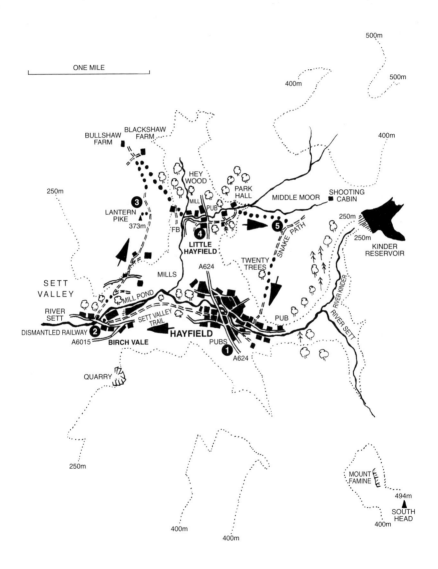

ONE MILE

500m
500m
400m
400m

BLACKSHAW
FARM
BULLSHAW
FARM
250m
HEY
WOOD
PARK
HALL
MIDDLE MOOR
SHOOTING
CABIN
MILL
PUB
LANTERN
PIKE
373m
FB
LITTLE
HAYFIELD
250m
250m
KINDER
RESERVOIR
SNAKE PATH
TWENTY
TREES
MILLS
A624
SETT
VALLEY
MILL POND
RIVER
SETT
SETT VALLEY
TRAIL
PUB
RIVER KINDER
RIVER SETT
DISMANTLED RAILWAY
A6015    BIRCH VALE
HAYFIELD
PUBS
A624
QUARRY

250m

MOUNT
FAMINE
494m
SOUTH
HEAD
400m
400m
400m

# THE WALK

1. From the bridge across the River Sett in the centre of Hayfield, head up along Church Street passing St Matthews' Church on your right immediately after which turn right (Bull's Head on corner) along a lane (SP 'Sett Valley Trail') and follow this straight on to quickly reach the main road (A624). Cross the road *(with care)* to join another road (bus turning circle and car park in front of you) where you turn left then almost immediately right along a lane into the Sett Valley Trail car park. Follow this lane straight on through the car park passing the toilet block/information centre on your right to reach a double gate at its far end *(start of the Sett Valley Trail)*. Head through the gate and follow the wide former railway track-bed straight on heading down the valley (SP 'Pennine Bridleway, Lantern Pike') through woodland for 1 mile to reach a road across the track. As you reach the road, turn right down along a roadside path ('Pennine Bridleway') to soon reach another gate at the end of the path that leads onto the road.

2. Turn right down along the road into the centre of Birch Vale, over a bridge across the River Sett and on passing a curving row of terraced houses (The Crescent) immediately after which turn right along a cobbled lane (SP 'Pennine Bridleway, Lantern Pike'). Follow this climbing quite steeply up at first passing behind The Crescent - the cobbles soon disappear and give way to a stony path which you follow steadily up to reach a bridlegate that leads onto a lane on a sharp bend. Follow this lane straight on (to the left) gently rising up to reach a road opposite a row of cottages. At the road, take the lane opposite to the right of the cottages (SP 'Pennine Bridleway, Lantern Pike') and follow this climbing steadily up (ignore the turning to the right after 250 yards) to reach a house at the end of the metalled lane. Bear to the right along the track passing in front of the house climbing steadily up along the stony track then, where this track forks, carry straight on up to reach a gate at on the edge of heather moorland (National Trust sign 'Lantern Pike'). Head through the gate and continue straight on along the track alongside the wall on

your right climbing gradually up across the eastern flanks of Lantern Pike. The track soon levels out then heads down, curving down to the right to reach a bridlegate at the end of the enclosed track at the bottom of the moorland. *(Short detour to the summit of Lantern Pike – where the track levels out, turn left along a narrow path through the heather which leads up to join a clearer path which you follow to the left to reach the summit. Re-trace your steps back down to the rough track).*

3. Head through the gate and follow the grassy track straight on across the field for 25 yards then, immediately after crossing a small stream, follow the indistinct grassy track bearing to the left across the middle of the field heading gently down to reach a junction of tracks and paths (and double wooden gate) in the bottom corner of the field (just above Blackshaw Farm). Do not head through the gates but turn right back on yourself (SP 'Hayfield via Little Hayfield') alongside the wall on your left (heading along the bottom edge of the field you have just walked across) and follow this wall to reach a stile in the bottom corner of the field. Cross the stile and follow the path bearing to the left down across the hillside alongside the wall/fence on your left, over another stile then along a clear enclosed path that slants down across the steep hillside to reach a track beside a house. At the track, cross the stile opposite and follow the path ahead gradually dropping down across the hillside then, as you reach the corner of the line of hawthorn trees (mill comes into view), follow the path to the left down across the hillside (following line of hawthorn trees) to join a stone-flagged path that leads down to reach a FB across a stream beside Clough Mill. Cross the FB and head up to join a road where you turn left passing Clough Mill on your left up through Little Hayfield to reach the A684 *(Lantern Pike Inn detour to left)*.

4. At the road, cross over *(take care)* and head along the stony lane opposite (National Trust sign 'Park Hall Woods') and follow this straight on through woodland (ignore any tracks off this lane). After about 0.25 miles the lane gently curves round to the left towards Park Hall then, as you approach the Old Stables (sign 'Residents Only beyond this point'), turn right along a rough track that quickly leads

to a gate at the edge of the woods. Head through the gate and follow the path directly ahead passing immediately to the left of the National Trust sign 'Middle Moor' and follow this narrow path heading steadily up across the heather moorland of Middle Moor for 0.5 miles to reach a wide track (Snake Path) and a wall across your path. Turn right along this track to soon reach a gate through the wall to your left.

5. Head through the gate and follow the track straight on, bearing left along the clearer track at the fork after about 50 yards and follow this curving round to the left across moorland to reach a metal kissing-gate beside a field gate in the bottom wall corner (end of the clear track). Head through the kissing-gate and follow the grassy path bearing slightly to the right gradually dropping down across the hillside (superb views) to join a wall on your right along the bottom of the field which you follow straight on to soon reach a metal kissing-gate beside a bridlegate through this wall to your right (near Twenty Trees). After the kissing-gate, follow the path to the left slanting down across the field through another kissing-gate, after which carry straight on down along the path which soon becomes a stony track that leads down to emerge between the houses onto Kinder Road on the edge of Hayfield. Turn right back into Hayfield.

# LONGNOR

*Longnor stands on a ridge of land between the upper Dove and Manifold valleys. The rivers are little more than trickling streams, but the valleys are broad with rich pastures hemmed in by rolling hills which makes for some of the finest walking in the Peak. That said, most people head further downstream to the limestone gorge of Dovedale leaving these upper reaches delightfully quiet. The River Dove forms the boundary between Derbyshire (east) and Staffordshire (west); this is also where the Dark Peak gritstone of the western moors meets the White Peak limestone of the southern dales. Longnor was first mentioned in the 13th Century, although there was almost certainly a village here before that as tradition states that it was burnt to the ground in Norman times in retribution for poaching deer in Leek Forest. Over the centuries, Longnor developed into a busy trading centre as it stood at the crossroads of several packhorse routes between the Potteries, the salt pans of the Cheshire Plain and towns such as Nottingham and Sheffield; some of these packhorse routes later developed into Turnpikes. Longnor's heyday was during the 18th and 19th Centuries when it developed into a small market town with over a dozen alehouses and a police station and lock-up to cope with the aftermath! However, the growth of the railways during the 19th Century heralded the demise of the packhorse and Turnpike routes leaving rural market towns such as Longnor to slowly decline. As such, Longnor remains remarkably untouched with many Georgian and Victorian buildings including the Market Hall of 1873 which overlooks the Market Place; note the list of tolls above the doorway by Order of Sir Vauncy Harpur-Crewe, Lord of the Manor. Other buildings of note include St Bartholomew's Church, a fine example of Georgian architecture, although a church has stood on this site since the 13th Century.*

## THE VILLAGE

Longnor boasts four pubs, B&B's, Post Office, general stores and newsagents, tea rooms, fish & chip shop, arts and craft shops, toilets, public payphone and a bus service.

## ACCOMMODATION

Tourist Information Centre, Buxton:     01298 25106

## LONGNOR PUBS

**Crewe & Harpur Arms, Longnor:**     **01298 83205**
This attractive brick-built Georgian coaching inn overlooks Longnor's old market place. Inside, there is a large, comfortable bar with a stone-flagged floor and imposing fireplace as well as a separate dining room.

**Grapes Hotel, Longnor:**     **01298 83802**
This small pub is tucked away in a corner of the cobbled market place, with one main bar warmed by an open coal fire.

**Horseshoe Inn, Longnor:**     **01298 83262**
This lovely three-storey stone-built pub dates back to 1609. Inside, the pub is warm and cosy with a quarry-tile floor, plenty of exposed stonework and a pot-bellied stove set in a through-fireplace.

**Ye Olde Cheshire Cheese, Longnor:**     **01298 83218**
Built in 1621 originally as a farmhouse although a pub since 1706 when it served travellers along the packhorse route between Cheshire and Yorkshire, hence its name. Inside, it boasts a warm and welcoming atmosphere and traditional surroundings with bench seating around a glowing coal fire.

## PUBS ALONG THE WALKS

Quiet Woman, Earl Sterndale:     01298 83211
New Inn, Flash:     01298 22941
Travellers Rest, Flash Bar:     01298 23695

# Longnor Walking Weekend
## - Saturday Walk -
### *Longnor, Shining Ford, Manifold Head, Flash & Dove Head*

## WALK INFORMATION

| | |
|---|---|
| Highlights | Walking up to Manifold Head, the highest village in Britain, 'flash Harry' spends his 'flash money', the five rivers of Axe Edge, an old packhorse bridge and walking down from Dove Head. |
| Distance | 11.5 miles          Time          6 hours |
| Maps | OS Explorer OL24 |
| Refreshments | Pubs, shops and cafés at Longnor. Pub at Flash. Pub and shop at Flash Bar. Café at Hollingsclough village hall (summer Sundays only). |
| Terrain | This walk follows indistinct paths across rough undulating fields for most of the way, passing through several farmyards (farm animals and sheep dogs). There are some short stretches of road walking around Longnor, Fawfieldhead, Flash and Hollinsclough. Many of the paths are boggy underfoot particularly around Shining Ford, between Marnshaw Head and Flash as well as the riverside path along the wooded banks of the Dove. |
| Ascents | Flash - 470 metres above sea level. |
| Caution | There are a number of short but steep sections along this walk as well as numerous stiles. Take care when walking along roads, as well as crossing the A53 at Flash. Navigation is quite complex due to the numerous farms, side valleys and unfrequented paths. |

# POINTS OF INTEREST

One of Staffordshire's great rivers, the Manifold rises on the flanks of Axe Edge, less than half a mile away from the source of the River Dove. Five rivers rise on the flanks of Axe Edge - the Dove, Manifold, Dane, Goyt and Wye - with three flowing into the North Sea and two into the Irish Sea. From its source, the Manifold is gentle and serene, little more than a stream meandering through a shallow valley criss-crossed by hedgerows and dotted with farms until it reaches Hulme End where it undergoes a dramatic transformation. The sandstones of the Dark Peak are left behind and the river carves a gorge through the limestone of the White Peak, twisting and turning below towering outcrops and disappearing through underground passages before reappearing at Ilam just before its confluence with the River Dove. Our walk follows the Manifold from Longnor to its source near the village of Flash.

Flash is the highest village in Britain at 1,518-ft above sea level, with superb views across the Staffordshire Moorlands. There are higher settlements, but this is a proper village with a pub, church, Post Office, village hall, school and a cluster of cottages. This windswept village lies just below Oliver Hill, the highest ground in Staffordshire, and is renowned for its harsh winters. According to folklore, it was once a centre for the production of counterfeit money, which was distributed at nearby Three Shire Heads where the counties of Derbyshire, Staffordshire and Cheshire meet. This is where the term 'flash' comes from, as in 'flash Harry' or 'flash money', a by-word for sharp practice.

Just beyond the Travellers Rest at Flash Bar lies the source of the River Dove, with Axe Edge rising above. From the bridge at Dove Head, the river flows through a dramatic ravine that is far grander than this stream deserves! Footpaths and old packhorse trails thread their way down through this narrow valley, which only begins to open out as it approaches Hollinsclough. Look out for the packhorse bridge beside an ancient ford situated in a delightfully secluded spot known as Washgate.

*For more information about Chrome Hill & Hollinsclough, see Sunday Walk.*
*For more information about the River Dove, see Walking Weekend 6 & 11.*

# LONGNOR SATURDAY WALK

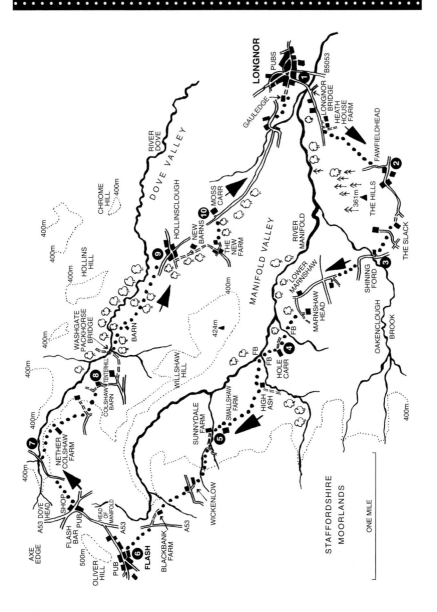

# THE WALK

1. From Longnor's Market Place (with your back to the Market Hall), turn right to quickly reach a crossroads where you head straight on along Leek Road and follow this down out of the village to reach Longnor Bridge across the River Manifold. Cross the bridge and continue up along the road to reach Heath House Farm on your left. Continue along the road passing the farm (ignore tracks into farmyard) then, just after you have passed the farm buildings, cross the wall-stile to the left (SP). After the stile, head straight down across the field (farm buildings to your left) walking parallel to a track on your left down into the bottom of a 'dip' (markerpost) where you bear slightly to the right up to reach a wall corner. Cross the stile just up from this wall corner (SP), then bear left slanting up across the middle of the field passing a wall corner jutting out into the field (markerpost) to reach a wall-stile, after which bear right to reach a gate in the field corner that leads onto a road. Turn left along the road to soon reach a junction in the hamlet of Fawfieldhead.

2. Turn right along the road and follow it passing Fawfieldhead Farm after which the road drops down for 0.25 miles and curves to the right then, as it curves to the left, cross the stile to the right just after a farm track. After the stile, follow the track ahead to reach a stile beside a gate that leads into the farmyard of The Slack. After the stile, head right passing to the right side of the barns to reach a wall-stile that leads out onto a field. Head straight on alongside the wall on your right and over a wall-stile then head down to join a lane. At the lane, take the FP opposite (SP) and head straight down across three fields through a series of wall-gates to reach Shining Ford (house). As you reach the house, bear left alongside the fence (and gardens) on your right to join a road beside the entrance to the house. Turn right along the road down over a bridge across Oakenclough Brook.

3. After the bridge, follow the road rising up and bending round to the left then turn right along an enclosed grassy path (SP). Follow this path down into a dip (boggy) then up to join a lane on a bend beside

the entrance to a farmhouse, where you head straight on to reach a road junction. At the junction, turn left then immediately right along a lane ('Dead End' sign) and follow this straight on for just over 0.25 miles then bending sharp left just after Lower Marnshaw Head cottage and continue along the lane to reach its end beside the entrance to Marnshaw Head Farm. At this farm entrance, head right over a wall-stile beside a gate (SP) then straight on to quickly reach another wall-stile/gate on the brow of a hill (Manifold Valley). After this stile, head straight down the hillside and over a wall-stile in the middle of the wall at the bottom of the field (ignore stile to the right in a 'dog-leg' along the wall). After this stile, bear slightly left down across the rough hillside *(heading towards farm buildings ahead sheltered by trees)* to reach a stile and a small plank FB across a stream at the bottom of the field just to the left of the line of trees along the banks of the stream. After the stile, head straight on alongside the fence on your right heading towards Hole Carr Farm then, as you approach the top of the field (farm just ahead), cross the stile to your right just before the corrugated barn, after which turn to the left around the barn and over another stile onto a track. Turn left along the track to reach a wall-stile that leads into the farmyard of Hole Carr Farm.

4. As you enter the farmyard, head over the wall-stile just to your right that leads out onto a field then walk straight on alongside the wall on your right down to reach a stile beside a gate, after which drop down a grassy bank to reach a FB across a stream *(with another FB just ahead across the River Manifold)*. Cross this first FB and walk straight on for a short distance then cross the wall-stile to the left of the gate (ignore FB across the Manifold just to your right). After the wall-stile, bear right up across the rough field to reach a gap in a tumbledown wall beside a telegraph pole in the middle of the field (SP) where you head straight on along a grassy track to reach a stile/gate beside High Ash Farm. After the gate, head straight on alongside the fence on your left to reach a gate near a barn where you turn right (SP 'Flash') up along the field boundary on your left all the way to reach a stile over a fence in the top corner of the field. After the stile, head straight on alongside a tumbledown wall on your left

and over a stile across a fence, then bear very slightly to the left across the field passing to the right of a small barn to reach Smallshaw Farm. As you approach the farm, pass to the right of the buildings and large barn (do not enter the farmyard) to reach a stile over a fence, after which cross another stile just ahead then bear slightly left down across the rough field towards Sunnydale Farm to reach a bridlegate beside a field gate (pond on your right) that leads into the farmyard.

5. As you enter the farmyard, follow the gravel track to the left (SP) leaving the buildings behind and follow this gently rising up for a further 100 yards then, where the track bends up to the left (with a gate and track off to the right), head straight on up alongside the fence on your right leaving the track to curve away (sign on fence 'footpath to Wickenlow'). Follow this fence up to reach a gate across your path, after which walk straight on alongside a fence/stream on your right that leads up over a stile across a tumbledown wall, after which carry straight on for a further 150 yards then cross the stream to the right and head up across the field to reach Wickenlow (bungalow). Cross the stile beside the gate just to the left of the bungalow that leads into the yard where you head straight on along the track up to join a road opposite a house. At the road turn left then immediately right over a stile beside a gate (SP) that leads onto the driveway of the house where you head up over the stile just to the left of the house. After the stile, head straight on across the rough field bearing slightly to the right keeping close to the wall/fence on your right at first then, where this fence bends away, head down to a stile in a fence across your path. After the stile, bear slightly to the right down the hillside *(heading towards farmhouse on hillside opposite)* and over a small FB across a stream, then head up to the right across the hillside towards Blackbank Farm and over a stile across a fence just before the farmhouse. After the stile, turn right and cross another stile that leads into the farmyard in front of the farmhouse where you head straight on along the lane up to join the A53. At the road take the FP opposite over a stile beside a gate (SP), after which head to the right alongside the wall on your right and follow this along the edge of three fields over two more stiles *(heading towards Flash)* to

reach a stile beside a gate that leads into farmyard on the edge of Flash (large barns across to your left). After the gate, bear up to the left through the farmyard along the rough track passing to the right-side of the large barn (churchyard on your right) and follow this into the centre of Flash.

6. Turn right along the road passing the church on your right and follow this out of Flash to reach the A53, where you turn left along the roadside path to reach the Travellers Rest at Flash Bar. Take the turning to the right towards 'Longnor' immediately after the pub then, after a short distance, take the FP to the left over a stile beside a gate (SP). Head straight on passing to the right-side of the barn and down over a stile across a fence, after which head straight down the hillside alongside a shallow dip/stream on your right to soon reach a rough track across your path. Cross over the track onto the right-hand side of the stream and follow this down across the hillside, bearing very gradually to the right away from the stream to reach a track at the bottom of the field which you follow to the right to join a road. Turn left down the road to reach a bridge across the River Dove at Dove Head.

7. Take the FP to the right immediately before this bridge and follow the path straight on with the river to your left heading alongside the wall on your right along the top of a low bank up to reach a stile at the end of this short section of wall (by a telegraph pole). Cross the stile and walk straight on (to the left) along the top of the bank following a line of telegraph poles (River Dove down to your left) to reach another stile in a wall corner. After this stile, carry straight on alongside the wall/fence on your left and follow this curving to the right (Nether Colshaw Farm just ahead to your right) to reach a stile to your left before a gate in the field corner. Cross the stile and turn immediately right alongside the field boundary on your right for 150 yards then, as you become parallel with the farmhouse up to your right, cross the stile to your right over the fence/tumbledown wall (beside a telegraph pole). After the stile, head left up across the field and over a stile halfway up the field, after which carry straight on gently bearing up across the hillside to reach a stile over a fence then

continue up across the next field to reach another stile *(views ahead of upper Dove Valley)*. After this stile, bear right across the field and through a gap in a wall then carry straight on to reach a stile in the bottom field corner that leads onto a lane on a bend. Cross over the lane and head through the metal gate opposite to the left (SP) - *ignore the bridlegate/stile to the right of this gate*. After the gate, walk straight down the field keeping close to the wall on your left then, as you approach the bottom of the field, follow this wall bending sharp left to quickly reach a small wall-gate that leads onto an enclosed grassy track. Turn right along this track down to reach a metalled lane beside the entrance to Colshaw Barn (house).

8. Head straight on (to the right) along the lane and follow it down into a small 'dip' then on to reach a T-junction with another lane. Turn left for a short distance then, as you reach the entrance to Tenterhill Farm, take the rough enclosed track to the right and follow this straight on then dropping down (rocky track) to reach a ford over a small stream just beyond which is a ford and packhorse bridge across the River Dove (Washgate). After the ford across the small stream, take the FP to the right over a stile across a fence (SP 'Hollinsclough') - *do not cross the packhorse bridge*. After the stile, follow the path turning to the right after a few paces over a slab FB across a small stream then carry straight on along the clear path keeping close to the wooded banks of the River Dove to your left. After a short distance, the path gently rises up across the wooded riverbank (Dove down to your left) then soon levels out and leads on across the steep wooded riverbank to reach a waymarker where you carry straight on (ignore grassy path branching up to the right) to emerge from the woodland. Carry straight on along the clear path *(valley opens out and the river curves away to the left)* gently rising up across the hillside to reach a stone barn. Pass to the left side of the barn and follow the grassy path gently rising up the hillside (row of hawthorn trees on your left) to reach another grassy path at the top of the hawthorns (by an old wall). Follow this path to the left heading across the hillside with the old wall on your left at first (Dove Valley down to your left) then gently rising up to join a tumbledown wall - follow the path straight on alongside this tumbledown wall

heading across the hillside, then drop down slightly through woodland and on to reach a stile. Cross the stile and follow the path straight on across the wooded hillside to soon emerge from the woods, where you carry straight on along a wide path across the hillside to reach the road just above Hollinsclough. Turn left down into Hollinsclough.

9. At the road junction in the centre of Hollinsclough take the stony track to the right just before the 'phone box and follow this up passing Home Farm on your left. About 25 yards after the barn the track forks - turn left up along a rough track which soon levels out and emerges from the woods. Follow this track straight on then climbing quite steeply up above New Barns Farm to the top of the bank, where you follow the track bending to the right to join a metalled lane beside the entrance to a farmhouse. Head straight on along this lane for about 25 yards then turn left along a walled metalled lane (SP) and follow this straight on then curving to the left into the farmyard of The New Farm. Head through the farmyard along the grassy track to the left of the garage that quickly leads to a stile beside a gate. Cross the stile and head straight on alongside the wall on your right to reach another stile in the wall corner, after which head straight down the hillside following the line of telegraph poles (wooded stream to your right) with a final steep descent to reach a stile at the bottom of the field that leads onto a road opposite Moss Carr Farm.

10. Turn right along the road for 1 mile to reach a T-junction. Turn left towards 'Longnor' and follow the road curving to the right up a steep hill then, half-way up this hill, cross the wall-stile to the right hidden in a hedge (SP). After the stile, head to the left along the broad, grassy path rising up to reach a squeeze-stile in a wall *(ignore squeeze-stile down to your right)*, after which head on alongside the wall on your left across the top of the field, through a squeeze-stile then on to reach a gate across your path (Gauledge Farm to your left). Head through the gate and bear left through a small wall-gate that leads onto a lane beside the farm entrance where you turn right back into Longnor.

# Longnor Walking Weekend
## - Sunday Walk -
### Longnor, Earl Sterndale, Chrome Hill & Hollinsclough

## WALK INFORMATION

Highlights    The upper Dove Valley, an unusual pub sign, an unlucky church, tropical reefs, the dragon's back and the hidden hamlet of Hollinsclough.

Distance    8.5 miles        Time        4 hours

Maps    OS Explorer OL24

Refreshments    Pubs, café and shops at Longnor. Pub at Earl Sterndale. Refreshments served at Hollinsclough Village Hall (summer Sundays only).

Terrain    This walk follows a mixture of clear field paths, quiet country lanes and stony farm tracks, with some short sections of road walking around Earl Sterndale, Hollinsclough and Yewtree Grange Farm.

Ascents    Hollins Hill (flanks of) - 400 metres above sea level.

Caution    This walk involves a number of short but quite steep sections including the descent from Hitter Hill and the descent into Dowel Dale. Take care along the stretches of road walking.

# POINTS OF INTEREST

The jagged crests of Parkhouse and Chrome hills dominate the upper Dove Valley. Chrome Hill, pronounced Croom, is derived from an Old English word meaning curved or sickle-shaped, an apt description for it has a mesmerising profile reminiscent of a dragon's back with bare rocks punctuating its curving narrow ridge. These hills are limestone reef knolls, formed 350 million years ago when this area was submerged under a tropical sea. Coral reefs developed on the fringes of this sea, which over millions of years built up to form a resistant limestone that has created these magnificent outcrops. These hills with their narrow serrated ridges are some of the only real peaks in the Peak District, as the name of this area is actually derived from the tribe who lived in this area during the Dark Ages known as the Pecsaetan or 'hill dwellers'.

Across the valley lies Earl Sterndale. Old cottages and farms look out across a village green with the battlemented tower of St Michael's Church rising above. This church has the unfortunate distinction of being the only church in Derbyshire to be hit by a German bomber during the Second World War. Across from the church stands The Quiet Woman, a classic Peakland pub that dates back to 1625. The pub sign depicts a headless woman above which is written *'Soft Words Turneth Away Wrath'*. Many years ago the landlord of the pub used to enjoy his regular trips to Longnor market where he would also frequent several pubs, arriving home worse for wear, much to the disdain of his wife. One evening, after a long day at Longnor, he returned home to be greeted by his ranting wife and so he cut off her head!

Across the valley lies the hamlet of Hollinsclough, an attractive cluster of old cottages, farms and the Bethel Chapel, built in 1801 by John Lomas, a hawker and jaggerman who made his money from the packhorse trade; jaggermen were the people who looked after trains of packhorses. Hollinsclough once stood at the junction of several important packhorse routes including a salt road from Cheshire into Derbyshire that crossed the Dove via a cobbled ford just to the north of the hamlet. Hollinsclough still boasts a village school, situated behind its 19th Century predecessor that is now used as an outdoor centre.

# LONGNOR SUNDAY WALK

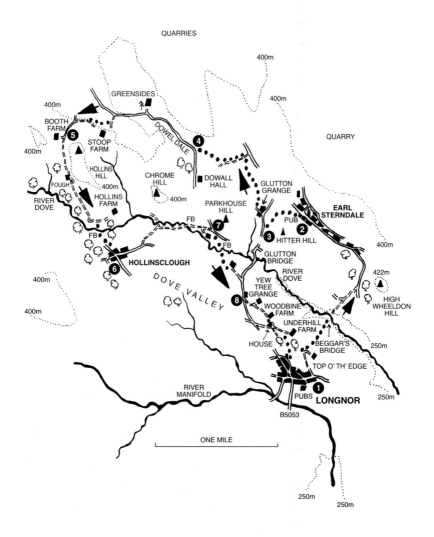

160

# THE WALK

1. From Longnor's Market Place (with your back to the Market Hall), turn left along the road passing the Olde Cheshire Cheese and follow this road up through the village. As you reach the last of the houses at Town Head take the lane to the left along Dove Ridge and follow this straight on then, beside the last of the houses on your left, follow the right-hand track over the brow of the hill (Top O' th' Edge) overlooking the Dove Valley (SP 'Bridleway'). Follow the track steeply down then, at the bottom of the hill where it bends round to the right towards the Water Treatment Works, take the track to the left off this bend beside a barn. Follow this track for a few paces then turn right through a gate immediately after the barn (SP). Head straight on across the field alongside the wall on your right then, where this wall ends (boggy ground), carry straight on across the middle of the field then drop down to reach Beggar's Bridge (FB) across the River Dove at the bottom of the field. Cross the FB and follow the grassy track up through a gate and onto a lane, which you follow straight on up to quickly join a road *(High Wheeldon Hill in front of you)*. Turn left along the road and follow it up through a dry valley then curving up to the left. The road levels out and leads straight on into Earl Sterndale. Follow this road into the centre of the village to reach the Quiet Woman pub overlooking the green.

2. Take the FP to the right of the Quiet Woman pub and follow it to the left around the buildings then immediately right (SP 'Hollinsclough') through the yard to quickly reach a stile just behind a house. Cross the stile then head straight on through two small wall-gates and out onto a field, where you bear slightly left across the field passing to the left of a wall-corner down to reach a gate in the bottom corner of the field *(Parkhouse Hill ahead)*. Head through the gate then walk across the next field and over a wall-stile, after which follow the path winding down across the steep hillside to reach a wall-stile then bear left across the field to join the road through a small gate at the foot of Parkhouse Hill (SP).

3. Turn right along the road for a short distance then, as it bends to the right in front of Glutton Grange Farm *(three-storey farmhouse dated 1675)*, turn left through the farmyard through a gate between the farmhouse and some barns. Follow the track up to reach three gates at the end of the track where you turn right through a gate (SP). Follow the grassy track heading up through the limestone valley keeping close to the wall on your left and follow this steadily up (following line of telegraph poles) to eventually reach a wall-stile in the top corner of the field that leads onto a track. Cross the track over the stile opposite then turn immediately left heading up alongside the field boundary/track on your left to reach a wall-stile beside a gate in the top corner of the field. Cross the stile and head straight on across the middle of the field to reach another stile above Dowel Dale, after which drop steeply down to join the road along the valley floor.

4. Turn right along the road up through Dowel Dale, over a cattle grid across the road at the head of the valley after which continue along the road passing a deep shake hole on your left then curving round to the left passing the entrance to Greensides Farm up to reach another cattle grid. Continue up along the road for a further 300 yards then, where the road bends right, turn left along a track (SP). Follow this track straight on to soon reach a cattle grid, immediately after which turn right (SP 'Booth Farm') across the field (markerposts) passing above Stoop Farm then drop down to join a track on your left which you follow straight on to quickly reach a stile over a fence beside this track. Cross the stile and follow the track to reach a road where you turn left to reach a fork in the road at the entrance to Booth Farm.

5. Head straight on over a cattle grid *(do not head down to Booth Farm)* and follow this track across the flanks of Hollins Hill curving round to reach Fough Farm. As you reach this farmhouse the track forks - follow the left-hand track straight on passing to the left of the farmhouse, just after which the track forks again. Follow the right-hand track gradually slanting down across the hillside (Dove Valley down to your right) to reach a gate across the track, after which

follow the track curving round to the left then take the FP off to the right down across the wooded hillside to reach a small metal gate in the bottom field corner that leads down over a FB across the Dove beside a cobbled ford. After the FB, follow the path slanting to the left up across the hillside, which soon becomes an enclosed path that leads up through a bridlegate and onto the road. Turn left down into Hollinsclough.

6. At the road junction in the heart of Hollinsclough, turn left passing the old schoolhouse (small white bell-tower) and follow this lane down out of the village, curving round to the left then take the farm track to the left over a cattle grid passing a stone barn ('Hollins Farm' sign). Follow this track straight on across fields to reach a fork in the track just above the banks of the River Dove *(Chrome Hill above)*. Turn right at this fork and follow the track along the banks of the Dove on your left to reach a ford/FB across the river. Cross the FB and carry straight on along the track to soon join the driveway leading to The Stannery where you continue straight on to join an unfenced road at the foot of Parkhouse Hill. *Access Land to the top of Parkhouse Hill.*

7. Turn right along the road for a few paces and take the FP to the right (SP) then bear slightly left across the field to reach a FB across the River Dove, after which follow the path to the left (stony at first then grassy) heading up across the hillside to reach a squeeze-stile just above a farmhouse. Follow the enclosed path straight on to quickly join the farm lane where you turn right to reach the main road. Turn right up along the road (take care) passing a house on your left, just after which take the farm lane to the left (just before the traffic lights) down towards Yew Tree Grange Farm.

8. Follow this lane down then, as you reach the farm, follow the right-hand lane passing above the farm buildings to soon reach a stile beside a cattle grid at the entrance to Woodbine Farm. Cross the stile and follow the enclosed path straight on alongside the driveway to reach the farmhouse. Follow the grassy track passing to the right side of the farmhouse for a short distance then, just before a gate, follow

the path up to the right over a stile. After the stile, turn left up to join a track below another house, which you follow up to quickly reach a junction of tracks in front of the house. Take the first track to the left (SP) and follow this down to reach a gate in a wall across the track *(Underhill Farm just ahead)*, immediately after which turn right through a squeeze-stile then follow the path up the wooded hillside (stone steps at first then a grassy path) to reach a wall-stile at the top of the bank. Cross the stile and walk straight on bearing very slightly left to join a wall on your left, which you follow straight down to reach a stile in the bottom field corner beside some houses on the edge of Longnor. Cross the stile and follow the wall on your left (houses to your right) down to join a lane which you follow to the left back into Longnor.

*Longnor*

# TIDESWELL

*Tideswell, known locally as 'Tidza', feels more like a town than a village, mainly because this was once an important trading centre with a market charter dating back to 1251. The weekly markets are no more but the Market Square can be found at the top of the High Street whilst the smaller Pot Market lies adjacent to the church. Some say its name is derived from the famous Ebbing and Flowing Well, one of the original 'Seven Wonders of the Peak' as described by Thomas Hobbes in 1636. However, this well is actually a few miles away in Barmoor Clough, although a spring in a garden along Manchester Road also claims the title. In reality, Tideswell takes its name from a Saxon farmer called Tidi. It remained a small farming community until the Norman Conquest when this area was given to William Peverel who built his castle overlooking present-day Castleton. In the Middle Ages Tideswell developed as a market centre for the southern part of the Royal Forest of the Peak, the hunting preserve administered from Peveril Castle, and it prospered from lead mining and wool. This wealth is reflected in the magnificent Church of St John the Baptist - the 'Cathedral of the Peak'. Built between 1350 and 1399, it is the most complete medieval church in the Peak District and a superb example of late Decorated Gothic and early Perpendicular architecture. Inside, the spacious nave and chancel are awash with wonderful carvings, brasses and memorials. In the churchyard lies William Newton, a self-educated poet who became known as the 'Minstrel of the Peak'. As the lead mines declined during the 19th Century, Tideswell lost some of its importance, which meant that the church was overlooked by Victorian 'improvers'.*

## THE VILLAGE

Tideswell offers pubs, B&B's, Youth Hostel (Ravenstor), fish & chip shop, cafés, delicatessen, small supermarket, greengrocers, butchers, newsagent, chemist, Post Office, NatWest bank, craft and gift shops, Library and Information Centre, bus service and toilets.

## ACCOMMODATION

Tourist Information Centre, Buxton:          01298 25106

## TIDESWELL PUBS

**George Hotel, Tideswell:**          **01298 871382**
Situated beside the church, this traditional coaching inn dates back to 1730 and is noted for its attractive stone frontage complete with Venetian windows. Inside, the comfortable lounge is made up of several inter-connecting rooms with lovely stone fireplaces. There is also a separate bar/games room.

**Horse & Jockey, Tideswell:**          **01298 872211**
This welcoming pub boasts a stone-flagged bar with a lovely cast-iron range, a lounge area with a beamed ceiling and wooden floorboards as well as an upstairs dining room with exposed stonework.

**The Star, Tideswell:**          **01298 872725**
Tucked away along the High Street in the historic heart of Tideswell, this popular locals' pub boasts a lively, traditional atmosphere with several cosy rooms served by a central bar.

## PUBS ON THE WALKS

Monsal Head Hotel, Monsal Head:          01629 640250
Red Lion Inn, Litton:          01298 871458
Anglers Rest, Miller's Dale:          01298 871323

# Tideswell Walking Weekend
## - Saturday Walk -
### *Tideswell, Litton Mill, Brushfield, Monsal Viaduct & Cressbrook Dale*

## WALK INFORMATION

| | |
|---|---|
| Highlights | Seven dales in a day, a cotton mill with a tragic tale, beautiful limestone landscapes, full steam ahead along the Monsal Trail and National Nature Reserves. |
| Distance | 9.75 miles          Time          4 hours |
| Maps | OS Explorer OL24 |
| Refreshments | Pubs, shops and cafés at Tideswell, Monsal Head and Litton. Café at Cressbrook Mill. |
| Terrain | From Tideswell, a path leads down through Tideswell Dale to reach Litton Mill from where there is a steep climb to join a track that leads to Brushfield. This track continues high above Monsal Dale before dropping steeply down to join the Monsal Trail beside Monsal Viaduct. This old railway line is followed up through the valley to reach Cressbrook Tunnel from where a path skirts across a steep hillside to reach Cressbrook Mill. A lane leads up to Ravensdale Cottages from where a muddy path heads up through Cressbrook Dale (nature reserve) before climbing out of the valley across fields to Litton. A country lane leads back to Tideswell. |
| Ascents | Priestcliffe Lees - 330 metres above sea level. |
| Caution | Steep sections include the climb from Litton Mill and the descent to Monsal Viaduct. There are steep drops to the side of the path as you approach Cressbrook Mill. Take care walking along the road between Litton and Tideswell. |

# POINTS OF INTEREST

The limestone side-valley of Tideswell Dale meanders southwards from Tideswell to join Miller's Dale near the former industrial hamlet of Litton Mill. Most of Tideswell Dale is owned by the National Park Authority who have transformed an old basalt quarry into a delightful nature reserve with riverside paths, woodland walks and a sculpture trail. The central stretch of the limestone gorge of the River Wye is known as Miller's Dale where road, railway, river, mill race and mill complex compete for space along the narrow valley floor. This river gorge is at its best between Litton Mill and Cressbrook Mill (known sequentially as Miller's Dale, Water-cum-Jolly Dale and Monsal Dale beyond Cressbrook Mill) with towering crags, steep slopes and wooded riverbanks teeming with wildlife. Litton Mill dates back to 1782 and was built in this remote valley to be close to water power but far away from the Luddites of the towns. During the early 19th Century, this old cotton mill became notorious for the cruel treatment of its child workforce by mill owner Ellis Needham, which came to light after former child apprentice Robert Blincoe published his story and shocked the nation. Poor and orphaned children were brought to this mill as cheap labour from London and were made to work long hours in terrible conditions with meagre food. Many children died of disease or ill treatment. The mill closed in the 1960's and has recently been converted into apartments, but a sense of sadness prevails.

From Litton Mill, a path climbs steeply up out of the valley across the Priestcliffe Lees nature reserve, with wonderful views back across the deep limestone valleys. At the top of the climb, the path skirts the remains of old lead mines before joining a track above the dry valley of High Dale that leads to the farming hamlet of Brushfield. This track then skirts high above the deep wooded valley of Taddington Dale and Monsal Dale with superb views towards the Iron Age hill-fort of Fin Cop across the valley. The views only improve as you begin the long descent down to the impressive Monsal Viaduct. The cinder track-bed of the former Midland Railway's London to Manchester route, now the Monsal Trail, leads up through the valley passing the site of Monsal

Dale Station before reaching the blocked-up Cressbrook Tunnel, where the path skirts across the steep hillside to reach the magnificent Cressbrook Mill*. This cotton mill was established in 1783 by Richard Arkwright, the 'Father of the Factory System', although the original mill burnt down just two years after it had been built and was replaced by what is known as the Old Mill. In 1815, a much larger mill (the 'Big Mill') was built by William Newton, 'Minstrel of the Peak' and mill manager. This magnificent Georgian building is capped by a small bell-cote that once summoned the children to work. Unlike neighbouring Litton Mill, Newton treated his child workforce relatively well with decent accommodation in a row of cottages behind the mill as well as schooling and even some time off on Sundays! Note the weir and mill pond just above the mill that was built to create a head of water to power the waterwheels; now an attractive lake that floods much of Water-cum-Jolly Dale. The mill closed in 1965 and has recently been converted into apartments.

To the north of Cressbrook Mill lies beautiful Cressbrook Dale, one of the five dales that make up the Derbyshire Dales National Nature Reserve. Beyond Ravensdale Cottages, this deep, steep-sided valley is thickly cloaked with semi-ancient ash woodland. It is a delight to walk through this world of dense trees, moss-covered walls, crystal-clear streams, wild flowers and birds. Further up, the woodland is left behind and the valley reveals itself in all of its glory with limestone grassland and steep scree slopes dotted with trees. Near the head of the valley (just beyond our route) is Peter's Stone, a large limestone rock that is slowly slipping down the hillside and was the site of the last gibbet in Derbyshire in 1815. Litton is situated on the limestone plateau high above Cressbrook Dale, a classic White Peak village. Attractive 18th Century farms and cottages crowd round a spacious tree-shaded green complete with ancient stepped cross and stocks overlooked by the Red Lion, one of Peakland's most authentic village pubs. Both Litton and Tideswell hold their famous well dressing ceremonies at the same time each June, amongst the finest in the Peak District.

*For more information about the Monsal Trail, River Wye & Well Dressings, see Walking Weekend 1.*

*Cressbrook Tunnel will re-open during 2011 as part of a new cycle route between Buxton and Bakewell.*

# TIDESWELL SATURDAY WALK

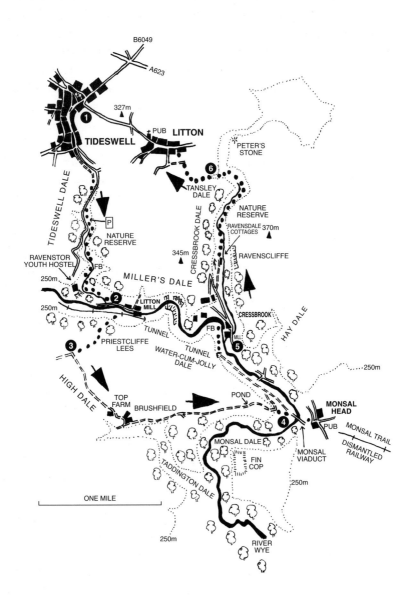

# THE WALK

**1.** From the small square in front of the main gates to Tideswell Church (with your back to the church) turn right along Commercial Road and follow this down through Tideswell passing the Horse & Jockey pub and then the piano-makers. Just before you leave Tideswell (where the houses on your left end) turn right up along Richard Lane for about 50 yards then take the FP to the left immediately before the playground (SP). Follow the track straight on through the stonemason's yard and continue along the walled track then, where the track forks (gate across the clearer track), follow the left-hand grassy track for a short distance then take the FP to the left through a small gate (SP). Head through the gate and follow the path to the right alongside the fence before slanting down the wooded hillside to join the road along the bottom of Tideswell Dale. Turn right along the road for 250 yards then take the FP branching off to the left (SP) which you follow heading down parallel to the road on your right to reach Tideswell Dale Car Park. Walk straight across the car park then along the clear, wide path at the other end - follow this alongside the stream heading down through Tideswell Dale for 1 mile to reach the road through Miller's Dale.

**2.** Turn left along the road to reach Litton Mill. As you enter the hamlet you pass a row of cottages on your left - just before these cottages end (with the entrance to Litton Mills just ahead), turn right along an enclosed FP (SP 'Monsal Trail to Miller's Dale') that leads across a FB over the River Wye, then winding steeply up the wooded hillside to reach the Monsal Trail (railway track-bed). Turn right then almost immediately left up steps beside the old railway bridge to reach a stile (Priestcliffe Lees Nature Reserve). Cross the stile and follow the path climbing steeply up the hillside, bearing very slightly to the right up to reach a stile beside a gate in the top right corner of this steep field. Head through the gate and continue up alongside the fence on your right to soon reach a stile across this fence. Cross the stile and follow the path up to the left then bear round to the right (path levels out) heading across a narrow field (overgrown workings) keeping close to the wall on your left to reach a gate at the top end of this narrow field that leads onto an enclosed track on a sharp bend.

3. Turn left along this track for 0.75 miles to reach the buildings of Top Farm just above the hamlet of Brushfield. Continue along the track skirting down around the large barns then carry straight on, leaving the farm buildings behind, along the metalled lane to reach the cluster of buildings at Brushfield (Middle and Lower farms). Follow the lane winding down then, where the lane forks just below the houses, turn left through a gate (SP 'Monsal Dale') and follow the lane through the farmyard (houses of Brushfield on your left) and through another gate leaving the houses behind. Follow this track straight on *(views down into Taddington Dale)* up to reach a fork in the track after 0.5 miles. Follow the left-hand track heading straight on (rutted track) alongside the wall on your right and through a gate in the field corner, after which continue straight on along a clearer track (still with the wall on your right) to reach another gate in the field corner. An enclosed stony track now leads straight on high above Monsal Dale for 0.3 miles to reach a gate at the end of the walled track (beside a pond). Continue straight on along the track and follow it as it gently curves to the right and slants down across the steep hillside into Monsal Dale then, where the track bends sharply down to the left, head straight on along a rough enclosed BW that leads down to join the Monsal Trail beside Monsal Viaduct. *Detour to Monsal Head Hotel: Turn right over the viaduct then, as you approach the blocked-up tunnel, follow the path to the left up across the wooded hillside to reach a junction of paths just below a road where you turn right up steps to the Monsal Head Hotel. Re-trace your steps back to Monsal Viaduct.*

4. As you reach the Monsal Trail beside Monsal Viaduct, turn left (away from the viaduct) and follow the track-bed straight on for 0.75 miles *(passing the former Monsal Dale Station along the way)* to reach a bridlegate to your right just before the blocked-up Cressbrook Tunnel*. Head through the bridlegate and follow the path across the

steep hillside passing above Cressbrook Mill, with the River Wye down to your right, then winding down rocky steps to reach a FB above the river just below the weir and mill pond. Cross the FB and follow the path straight on for a short distance then, where it forks, head right alongside the mill-race and follow the enclosed path to the left through the yard of Cressbrook Mill to join a road. *The four blocked-up old railway tunnels along the Monsal Trail, including Headstone Tunnel (Monsal Head), Cressbrook Tunnel, Litton Tunnel and Chee Tor Tunnel, will all re-open during 2011 as part of a new cycle trail between Buxton and Bakewell.*

5.  Turn left along the road then, where the road forks after a short distance, take the right-hand road towards 'Cressbrook, Litton'. Follow this road rising up for 0.3 miles to reach a turning to your right towards Ravensdale. Turn right and follow this lane down through woodland to reach Ravensdale Cottages. Carry straight on along the lane passing to the left of the cottages to reach the end of the road where you continue straight on along the enclosed path - follow this path through woodland heading up through Cressbrook Dale, with the stream on your right, to soon reach a FB across the stream (Nature Reserve sign). Cross the FB and continue along the path through woodland with the stream now on your left then, where the path forks after about 150 yards, follow the left-hand path with the stream just to your left heading up through the valley. The path soon emerges from the trees and the valley opens out - continue along the path following the valley as it gently sweeps round to the left (stream disappears) then, just before the valley curves to the right, cross the stepping stones to your left that lead to a wall-gate *(stream usually dry at this point)*.

6.  After the wall-gate, follow the grassy path straight up through the side-valley of Tansley Dale to reach a tumbledown semi-circular stone enclosure (and overgrown workings) at the head of this side-valley, where you follow the path up to the right to reach a stile in the wall corner. Cross the stile and follow the path to the right up across the field passing a wall corner (SP 'Litton') then continue up across the narrow field to reach a stile beside a gate in the top left corner

that leads onto an enclosed track. Turn left along the track for about 25 yards then cross the wall-stile to the right and head diagonally across the middle of the field to reach a wall-stile in the far left corner (beside a cottage) that leads onto the main road through Litton. Turn left along the road across the village green then, where the road forks by the stepped cross (Red Lion to your right) take the road to the right and follow this up passing Christ Church on your right and out of the village. Follow this road for 0.75 miles (ignore any turnings off) back to Tideswell.

*Tideswell*

# Tideswell Walking Weekend
# - Sunday Walk -
## Tideswell, Monk's Dale, Wormhill, Chee Dale
## & Miller's Dale Station

## WALK INFORMATION

| | |
|---|---|
| Highlights | The valley of the monks, the father of the canals, delightful Chee Dale, a railway hub, towering viaducts and an ancient corn mill. |
| Distance | 8.5 miles *(short route: 4 miles)*     Time  4 hours |
| Maps | OS Explorer OL24 |
| Refreshments | Pubs, shops and cafés at Tideswell. Pub at Miller's Dale. Refreshments available at Miller's Dale Station. |
| Terrain | From Tideswell, stony tracks lead across the limestone plateau over to Miller's Dale from where a path heads up through narrow Monk's Dale, with a wet and rocky section through dense woodland. From the head of the valley, a grassy track climbs up to reach Wormhill from where a path leads quite steeply down into Chee Dale. A riverside path leads downstream to reach Chee Dale Viaduct where there is a short but steep climb up to join the Monsal Trail (old railway), which is followed back to Miller's Dale. Field paths and quiet lanes lead back to Tideswell. |
| Ascents | Wormhill - 340 metres above sea level |
| Caution | The path through Monk's Dale is rocky and wet underfoot, which makes progress slow especially after heavy rain. There are a number of short but steep sections, particularly around Miller's Dale and Chee Dale. |

# POINTS OF INTEREST

The area between Tideswell Dale and Monk's Dale is classic White Peak country with a myriad of old tracks and drystone walls tracing across the windswept plateau like a huge cobweb. The hamlet of Miller's Dale lies wedged into the steep-sided valley of the Wye, also known as Miller's Dale. The Wye valley has something of an identity crisis for it changes name six times between Buxton and Bakewell! As the name implies, there has been a watermill here since Saxon times. Centuries ago, watermills were owned by the lords of the manor and the tenant farmers had to pay to have their corn ground in the landlord's mill. The present mill dates from 1860 and was used up until the 1920's; the old waterwheel can be seen near the Angler's Rest on a site used for milling for at least nine centuries. The south side of the valley is scarred by a huge limestone quarry that operated from the 1870's until 1930. The adjacent row of large stone-built limekilns were used to produce quicklime by burning the limestone with coal, which was then taken away by train to be used as a building material and in agriculture to 'sweeten' soil. Nature is slowly reclaiming these old quarry workings.

The former Miller's Dale Station dominates this part of the valley, its two huge viaducts rising high above the river. This was once a busy junction along the Midland Railway's London to Manchester main line. The station opened in 1863 with three platforms - two for the Manchester line and one for the Buxton branch line. Imagine the scene with express trains bound for London, goods trains loaded with quicklime from the quarries and local trains full of tourists heading to the spa town of Buxton. In 1905 the station was enlarged and a second viaduct built across the Wye beside the original viaduct. The railway between Matlock and Buxton succumbed to Beeching's axe in 1968, much of which has since been turned into the popular Monsal Trail walking route.

Monk's Dale is one of the five valleys that make up the Derbyshire Dales National Nature Reserve. When you walk up through this valley you feel as though you are walking through an ancient landscape for this is the 'dale that time forgot'! Its geology and location means that it is colder and and higher than other White Peak valleys, so plants and flowers from the last Ice Age such as the alpine cinquefoil still thrive here. Its southern half is composed of scrub woodland, grassland and scree slopes that support an abundance of wild flowers. The northern half is thickly cloaked with ash woodland where the moss-covered boulders and twisted boughs give it an eerie atmosphere. In the 12th Century, Monk's Dale was bequeathed to Lenton Priory by William Peverel, Norman lord of this whole area. They established a grange (monastic farm) at what is now Monksdale Farm and may have had a small chapel in this valley. It is said that a secret passage linked this chapel with Tideswell Church.

Wormhill lies in a hollow sheltered from the harsh winds that blow across the limestone plateau. It is an agricultural village with several farms, attractive cottages and an interesting church. St Margaret's Church stands back from the road surrounded by trees and gardens. The church was all but rebuilt in Victorian times, although the tower dates back some 700 years, the upper part of which was modelled on the famous Saxon church at Sompting in Sussex. On the village green is the Brindley Memorial Fountain in memory of James Brindley who was born at nearby Tunstead in 1716. From humble beginnings, he rose to become one of the greatest engineers of the Industrial Revolution and was known as the 'Father of the English canal system'. In 1761, he built the Bridgewater Canal between Worsley and Manchester, the first arterial canal that proved to be a commercial success and so ushered in the canal era. He engineered much of the canal network across England that played a pivotal role in providing cheap materials and transport during the early years of the Industrial Revolution. From Wormhill, a path leads down into Chee Dale, as these upper reaches of the Wye are known, a supremely beautiful valley that is thickly cloaked in woodland. A riverside path heads downstream to soon reach Cheedale Viaduct from where a sharp climb leads up to join the Monsal Trail. From here, it is full steam ahead along the old track-bed to Miller's Dale Station.

*For more information about the Monsal Trail & the River Wye,*
*see Walking Weekend 1.*

# TIDESWELL SUNDAY WALK

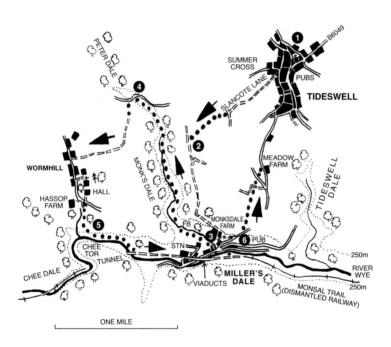

ONE MILE

# THE WALK

1. From the small square in front of the main gates to Tideswell Church (with your back to the church) turn right along Commercial Road and follow this bending to the right then left around NatWest Bank then, immediately after the bank, turn right up along Parke Road. Follow this lane up to reach a T-junction where you turn left then right after a short distance up along Summer Cross then immediately left along a stony track. Follow this track up passing an old mill on your right - the track climbs steadily up leaving the houses of Tideswell behind then levels out. Continue straight on along this walled track (Slancote Lane) for a further 0.5 miles to reach a junction of tracks (and gates) where the main walled track bends sharp left. Head straight on over the wall-stile beside the gate (SP) and walk straight down across the field and over a wall-stile tucked away beside a small 'dog-leg' in the wall at the bottom of the field. Cross the stile and walk straight on alongside the wall on your left to join a walled track across your path.

2. Turn left along this track and follow this to soon reach a junction with another track where you head to the right. Follow this clear track for a further 0.75 miles down to reach Monksdale Farm. Head through the gate behind the farmhouse that leads into the farmyard and follow the farm lane down to the right (SP 'Limestone Way') then, where this lane bends left after a short distance, head straight on along a stony track (SP 'Limestone Way') down to join a road. Turn right along the road steeply down to join the B6049 through Miller's Dale.

   *Short Route: As you reach the road just below Monksdale Farm, turn left up along the steep road then follow the route description from Point 6.*

3. Turn right along the B6049 for a short distance then take the enclosed FP to the right immediately after St Anne's Church. Follow this path up to reach a gate, after which head to the right over low limestone outcrops alongside a wall to quickly pick up a clear path

that leads down into Monk's Dale. Follow the streamside path through woodland to reach a FB. Cross the FB and follow the streamside path heading up through the wooded valley, with the stream now on your left. After a while, the valley opens out (steep, sparsely wooded pastures) and the path forks - follow the path over a small 'spur' of rock, which provides excellent views up the valley. The path soon joins the stream again and continues heading up following the valley as it sweeps round to the left - the steep valley sides soon crowd in and the path becomes rocky underfoot. The path then drops down onto the thickly wooded boulder-strewn valley floor. Progress is now slow as you pick your way over rocks beside the stream heading up through the wooded valley for over 0.5 miles to eventually reach a wall-stile beside a small overgrown pond at the end of the Nature Reserve. The path soon emerges from the trees and the valley opens out - continue straight on along the valley floor to reach a stile that leads onto the road.

4. Turn left along the road then, halfway up the hill, head left through a gate (SP 'Wormhill'). After the gate, bear slightly to the right up across the hillside to join a wall on your left which you follow up to quickly reach a bridle-gate in the top corner of the field. A walled path now leads up for 0.75 miles all the way to reach the road through Wormhill. Turn left along the road down through the village passing the Brindley Memorial Fountain and continue down along the road leaving Wormhill behind. Follow the road bending round to the left passing the entrance to Hassop Farm then, where the road straightens out (before the entrance to Wormhill Hall), take the track to the right (SP 'Chee Dale, Blackwell') down passing a cottage, after which a clear FP leads down through woodland (Nature Reserve) with a wooded ravine to your right. The path emerges from the woods onto a promontory of land high above Chee Dale where you follow the path round to the left then slanting down across the hillside to reach a FB across the River Wye.

5. Do not cross the FB but turn left along the riverside path (river on your right) heading down the valley for 0.25 miles to reach Cheedale Viaduct. Turn left before the viaduct steeply up steps to join the old

track-bed (Monsal Trail). Turn left and follow this track-bed straight on through woodland to reach the former Miller's Dale Station. About 100 yards before you reach the station car park, a path forks off to the right (SP 'Miller's Dale via river') - follow this path straight on passing the old station buildings and platforms then, just beyond the buildings, cross the right-hand of the two large viaducts spanning the River Wye gorge (SP 'Litton Mill, Bakewell'). After the viaduct, carry straight on along the track-bed for about 400 yards then take the FP to the left (SP 'Miller's Dale') down across a wooded bank before a stony path slants steeply down to reach a FB across the River Wye. Cross the FB to reach the road beside the Angler's Rest where you turn left to quickly join the B6049 opposite St Anne's Church. Turn right along the road for a short distance then take the turning to the left climbing steeply uphill.

6. Follow this road steeply up passing the entrance to Monksdale Farm (road levels out) after which continue along the road for about 75 yards then take the FP to the left over a wall-stile (SP). Head to the right up across the field to reach a stile near a gate in the top right corner, after which head straight up across the field and through a squeeze-stile, then straight on across the next field and through another squeeze-stile. After this stile, continue straight on alongside the wall on your left down to join a walled track. At the track, head straight on through the squeeze-stile and walk alongside the wall on your left down to join a road, where you take the FP opposite through a squeeze-stile and head straight on alongside the wall on your left down to join another road beside Meadow Farm. Turn left along this road and follow it rising up passing a group of barns after which the road levels out and leads back towards Tideswell. As you reach the outskirts of Tideswell you come to a T-junction where you turn right back into the village, taking any one of the numerous lanes down to the right back into the centre.

*The four blocked-up old railway tunnels along the Monsal Trail, including Headstone Tunnel (Monsal Head), Cressbrook Tunnel, Litton Tunnel and Chee Tor Tunnel, will all re-open during 2011 as part of a new cycle trail between Buxton and Bakewell.*

# WETTON

*Wetton is an unspoilt White Peak village of old cottages and farms grouped around a small green that is overlooked by a genuine village pub where you will find local farmers with local accents – a rarity in the Peak District! This quiet village is set in a shallow hollow beneath Wetton Hill, sheltered from the winds that blow across this broad limestone ridge between the Manifold and Dove valleys. Wetton was first settled in medieval times and takes its name from nearby Wetton Hill, which literally means 'wet hill'. The village was laid out to a plan by the lord of the manor with streets aligned in a grid pattern, although a glance at the map will reveal that the village never grew to fit its original planned layout – perhaps the landlord had ambitious plans for this village that never materialised. Such planned villages allowed the landlord to develop a more efficient system of agriculture based on strip farming where each villager was allotted some narrow pieces of land around the village. These were later enclosed by walls during the late 18th Century thus 'fossilising' this ancient farming system. In the 16th Century the Cavendish family of Chatsworth House, later the Dukes of Devonshire, became lords of the manor; indeed, their influence can still be felt today with a number of properties throughout the village. St Margaret's Church stands in the heart of the village, a small country church that dates back to medieval times. It was almost completely rebuilt in 1820 in simple and rather plain late Georgian style, although the tower retains medieval stonework. It is a delight to walk around the streets to admire the vernacular architecture including some fine old farm buildings; little has changed here for centuries.*

## THE VILLAGE

Wetton offers two B&B's, campsites, self-catering accommodation, toilets, phone box, bus service, car park and the Olde Royal Oak.

## ACCOMMODATION

Tourist Information Centre, Ashbourne:     01335 343666

## WETTON PUB

**Olde Royal Oak, Wetton:**     **01335 310287**
This lovely, welcoming village pub oozes character, especially the cosy bar with its tiled floor, low beams and open fire. There is a separate bar/lounge with a wooden floor as well as a sun lounge and attractive beer garden. Self-catering accommodation is available as well as a campsite behind the pub.

## PUBS ON THE WALKS

Izaak Walton Hotel, Ilam:            01335 350555
Watts Russell Arms, Hopedale:        01335 310126

# Wetton Walking Weekend
## - Saturday Walk -
### *Wetton, the Manifold Valley, Ilam, Dovedale & Hopedale*

## WALK INFORMATION

| | |
|---|---|
| Highlights | A surprise view, old lead mines and a nature reserve, a grand Youth Hostel, Saxon crosses, England's loveliest valley, queuing to cross the stepping stones and towering limestone pinnacles. |
| Distance | 9.5 miles          Time          4 - 5 hours |
| Maps | OS Explorer OL24 |
| Refreshments | Pubs at Wetton, Ilam and Hopedale. Cafés at Ilam Hall & Dovedale. |
| Terrain | Field paths lead all the way to Ilam, with an exhilarating path along the rim of the Manifold Valley. From Ilam, field paths lead across the flanks of Bunster Hill to join a track that leads up to reach the stepping-stones across the River Dove. A clear path then leads up through Dovedale for 1.25 miles before turning up through the side-valley of Hall Dale (rocky path) to reach Stanshope. A quiet lane is then followed before dropping down across fields to Hopedale from where field paths and quiet lanes lead back to Wetton. |
| Ascents | Wetton Low - 315 metres above sea level |
| Caution | There are steep drops to the side of the path along the rim of the Manifold Valley. Do not explore the old mine workings. The path through Dovedale may be muddy after rain. The path up through Hall Dale is quite steep and rocky underfoot. |

From Wetton, a footpath crosses narrow fields before skirting across the flanks of Wetton Low, with its prehistoric tumulus and fine views back towards the village, to reach the rim of the Manifold Valley and one of those 'wow' moments! This footpath then traces a high-level route along this rim passing the old lead mine workings of Bincliff Mine and then Highfields Mine that scar the steep wooded hillside with their overgrown waste tips. This area is not only of archaeological importance but also forms the Castern Wood Nature Reserve with over 240 species of plants recorded. For most of the year the riverbed between Wetton Mill and Ilam Park is dry as the River Manifold charts a subterranean course through caves and water channels in the limestone bedrock before reappearing several miles downstream in the grounds of Ilam Hall at the Boil Holes; only after prolonged rain does it flow above ground. Note the well-preserved medieval ridge and furrow ploughing strips across Ilam Park with their characteristic 'S' shape caused by the ox and plough as they turned around. Ilam Hall was originally built in around 1600 by the influential Port family who owned the estate until 1804 when it was sold to David Pike-Watts, a wealthy brewer. When his daughter Mary inherited the estate, her husband Jesse Watts-Russell rebuilt much of the Hall in Gothic baronial style during the 1820's. In the early 20th Century it was run as a hotel and restaurant but that proved unsuccessful and so it was sold to a demolition contractor. Thankfully, much of the building was saved by Sir Robert McDougall, the flour magnate, who bought it and gave it to the National Trust in 1934 on the understanding that it would be used as a Youth Hostel.

Just down from Ilam Hall stands the Church of the Holy Cross, which boasts a wealth of Saxon treasures including a doorway, ornate preaching crosses and a font with detailed carvings thought to depict the life of St Bertram, whose tomb can be found in the South Chapel. Bertram was an 8th Century Mercian prince whose wife and baby were killed by wolves in a nearby forest. Following this tragic event, he became a hermit who performed miracles. The church is a delightful mix of architectural styles including Saxon, Norman, Early English and Victorian Gothic. Up until the 1820's the village of Ilam surrounded this church but the village was rebuilt further away to improve the view from the Hall! The 'new' village of Ilam has a wonderful setting near the confluence of the rivers Manifold and Dove beneath the rounded bulk of Bunster Hill, which provides the perfect backdrop for the cluster of Alpine-style houses. Commissioned by Watts-Russell, these ornate estate houses were designed by Sir George Gilbert. In the centre of the village is the large Memorial Cross erected in memory of Mary Watts-Russell who died in 1840 aged only 48.

*"There are prospects in Derbyshire rivalling those of Switzerland and Greece"* remarked Byron in 1798, since when Dovedale has been one of the most celebrated and visited beauty spots in England, attracting around 2 million visitors each year! The jaws of Dovedale are guarded by the twin grassy hills of Thorpe Cloud and Bunster Hill, and anticipation grows as you follow the track up to reach the stepping-stones, which is as far as most of the 2 million visitors walk! More is the pity for the scenic delights of Dovedale are to be found upstream of these stepping stones with limestone pinnacles, most of which are named, as well as caves and ash woodland all set within this deeply incised river valley. A riverside path soon leads up to the promontory of Lover's Leap, with fine views towards the Twelve Apostles across the valley. Further up are the Tissington Spires then the natural arch of Reynard's Cave after which the path drops down to river level along a section known as The Straits before reaching the footbridge beside the twin pinnacles of Pickering Tor on the Derbyshire (east) side of the river and Ilam Rock on the Staffordshire (west) side. Dovedale only stretches for about three miles from Milldale to Thorpe Cloud, even though the River Dove actually flows for some 45-miles.

*For more information about the River Dove, see Walking Weekend 6.*

# WETTON SATURDAY WALK

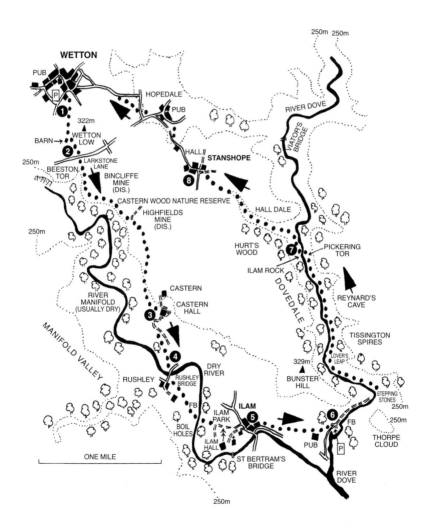

# THE WALK

**1.** From the road junction in the centre of Wetton (with your back to the Royal Oak) turn right down along the road towards 'Alstonefield, Ilam' and, at the bottom of the village, take the turning to the right towards 'Grindon (Manifold Valley)' then almost immediately turn left along a short stretch of grassy track to reach a squeeze-stile (SP). After the stile, bear right up across the small field through a wall-gate towards the top right corner, after which head left up across the field and through another small wall-gate (half way up the field), after which continue bearing up across the field to reach a wall-stile in the top corner. After this stile, continue up across the field heading towards the stone barn then, as you approach the top corner of the field (just beyond the large solitary tree but before the barn), cross the wall-stile to your left just before a wall corner. After the wall-stile, head down alongside the wall on your right to reach Larkstone Lane.

**2.** At the road take the FP opposite (SP 'Highfields Mine, Castern') and head straight on through a squeeze-stile, after which follow the path bearing to the right across the hillside alongside the wall on your left then straight on to reach a wall-stile *(Manifold Valley down to your right)*. Cross the wall-stile and follow the path straight on across the top of the steep hillside high above the Manifold Valley to reach a stile over a fence across your path (just beyond a promontory of land). Cross the stile and carry straight on along the top of the steep wooded bank gently rising up to reach a small gate in a fence/tumbledown wall, after which bear left up to quickly reach a squeeze-stile beside a gate, near a Castern Wood Nature Reserve sign. Head through the squeeze-stile then follow the FP to the right (SP 'Castern') through an area of old mining debris to quickly reach a field gate, after which head across the middle of the field bearing very slightly to the right to reach a field gate in the far corner. Head through the gate and walk straight on across the middle of the field gently dropping down then along an indistinct grassy track across the top of a low 'ridge' (medieval ploughing terrace) to a gate in the far bottom corner of the field. Head through this gate and follow the grassy track straight on keeping close to the wall on your right, through a gate across your path after which carry straight on along the stony track (wall still on your right) curving round to reach a metalled lane near the buildings of Castern Hall.

3. Turn right along the metalled lane (SP 'Ilam'), over a cattle grid then bending round to the right skirting around the buildings. Continue along the lane passing the entrance gates to Castern Hall and follow this lane winding down the hillside then, where the lane begins to level out, branch off to the right along a grassy path (markerpost). Follow this path gradually bearing away from the lane heading down across the hillside *(heading towards the two large farms on the hillside ahead)* to reach a squeeze-stile beside a field gate hidden amongst trees. After the squeeze-stile, head to the right down across the field through a gateway in a hedge then on across the next field to join the road beside Rushley Bridge across the River Manifold.

4. Turn right along the road across the bridge and over a cattle grid then, 25 yards after the cattle grid (as you approach the farm buildings), take the FP to the left through a small gate in a fence beside a field gate (SP). After the gate, head straight on up through another small gate then carry straight on up across the field to reach a large gap in a wall. After the wall gap, walk straight across the field and through a gate in a hedge then continue on gently dropping down across the field through a squeeze-stile, after which bear left down to reach a FB across the (dry) River Manifold. After the FB, forsake the gravel path and head straight up the grassy bank ahead bearing very slightly to the right then, at the top of the bank, head straight across Ilam Park *(ploughing strips)* to reach a stony/grassy track across the Park. Turn left along this track and follow it all the way to reach the road through Ilam village.

5. Turn right down along the road to reach the road junction beside the Memorial Cross where you turn left towards 'Dovedale, Thorpe'. Follow this road bending round to the right alongside the River Manifold for a short distance then, just after you have left the village, take the FP to the left through a gate in a fence (National Trust sign

'Bunster Hill'). After the gate, head to the right up to quickly join a stony track which you follow to the right across the hillside to reach a gate (end of the track). After the gate, head straight on bearing very slightly to the left across the field and through a bridlegate/field gate beside a 'junction' of hedges and fences (100 yards to the left of the farm buildings). Head through the gate and walk straight across the field and over two wall-stiles (about 50 yards to the left of the farm buildings), after which carry straight on down across the field bearing very slightly to the left heading towards the 'jaws' of Dovedale with Thorpe Cloud rising above *(Izaak Walton Hotel detour to the right over a stile)* to reach a stile that leads into woodland. Follow the path down through the belt of woodland to join a track, which you follow to the left to quickly reach a metalled lane beside Dovedale car park.

6. Turn left along the metalled lane ('No Vehicles' sign) and follow this up through Dovedale alongside the River Dove on your right for 0.3 miles to reach the stepping-stones *(if the river is in spate then use the FB downstream towards the car park)*. Cross the stepping-stones then turn left through a squeeze-stile/gate (SP 'Milldale') after which follow the clear riverside path straight on heading up through Dovedale. The path leads along the wooded riverbank at first then climbs up stone steps to reach the outcrop of Lover's Leap (viewpoint) before dropping down steps back to river level. Continue straight on along the clear path passing below the Tissington Spires (limestone pinnacles) then the arch of Reynard's Cave after which follow the riverside path heading up through the wooded valley to reach a FB across the river beside the limestone pinnacles of Pickering Tor (east riverbank) and Ilam Tor (west riverbank) - *this FB is 1.25 miles upstream from the stepping stones.*

7. Cross the FB (SP 'Stanshope') and turn immediately right along the wooded riverbank (river to your right) to reach a squeeze-stile, after which turn left (SP 'Stanshope') heading up through the side-valley of Hall Dale. The path leads steeply up at first through the narrow, rocky valley and over a stile, after which the valley soon opens out slightly - carry straight on along the clear path heading up along the

floor of this steep-sided valley for just over 0.5 miles to reach a small wall-gate at the head of the valley. After the wall-gate, head straight on to quickly reach another wall-gate, after which carry straight on keeping close to the wall on your left to reach a squeeze-stile in a wall across your path (ignore stile to left just before this). After this squeeze-stile, head straight on across the field *(Stanshope ahead)*, over a wall-stile then head to the right to join a walled track on the edge of Stanshope. Turn left along the track to reach the road through Stanshope beside a road junction/triangular green.

8. Follow the road to the right (ignore the turning to the right) and follow this curving round to the left (passing Stanshope Hall on your right) out of Stanshope. Head straight on along the road leaving the hamlet behind then, after about 0.25 miles, follow the road bending to the left then heading down passing a house on your left a short distance after which take the FP to the right through a squeeze-stile (just after the FP on your left). Head down through the shallow valley to quickly reach a wall-gate that leads onto a road where you turn left into the hamlet of Hopedale. Take the turning to the left just after the Watts Russell Arms towards 'Wetton, Ilam, Dovedale, Stanshope' and follow this road up to soon reach a road turning to your left where you take the FP to the right through a squeeze-stile. Bear left up across the field and through two squeeze-stiles and onto a road. Cross the road and take the FP opposite, after which bear right up across the field towards the top right corner to reach a squeeze-stile in the wall on your right that leads onto a road. Turn left along this road, bearing left at the fork after 0.25 miles back up into Wetton.

# Wetton Walking Weekend
## - Sunday Walk -
### Wetton, Ecton Hill, the Manifold Way, Wetton Mill & Thor's Cave

## WALK INFORMATION

| | |
|---|---|
| Highlights | Rich copper pickings, an Indian railway, a delightful mill, the valley of many folds and Thor's Cave. |

| | | | |
|---|---|---|---|
| Distance | 6.5 miles | Time | 3 hours |

| | |
|---|---|
| Maps | OS Explorer OL24 |
| Refreshments | Pub at Wetton. Café at Wetton Mill. |
| Terrain | Clear field paths and quiet country lanes lead from Wetton to the rim of the Manifold Valley on the flanks of Ecton Hill. A narrow path then traverses this steep hillside, with a short but particularly steep and narrow section before slanting down to reach the hamlet of Ecton and the Manifold Way. This old track-bed, now a metalled lane, leads down the valley passing Wetton Mill to reach a bridge across the river below Thor's Cave. A clear path (stone steps) leads steeply up through woodland out of the valley back to Wetton. The detour to Thor's Cave follows a clear woodland path that is quite steep in places. |
| Ascents | Ecton Hill - 350 metres above sea level |
| Caution | The section across the flanks of Ecton Hill above the Manifold Valley follows a narrow path across a very steep hillside - take care on this section. The section of the Manifold Way from Swainsley Tunnel to beyond Wetton Mill is also used by the occasional car. Take care if exploring Thor's Cave as the sloping rock is slippery. |

# POINTS OF INTEREST

To the north of Wetton lie a range of grassy limestone hills that mark the boundary between the limestone of the White Peak and the shales and sandstones of the Dark Peak. Of particular note is Wetton Hill, from where there are wonderful views across the upper reaches of the Dove and Manifold valleys with the wilds of Axe Edge and the Staffordshire Moorlands on the horizon. From the scattered hamlet of Back of Ecton, a path leads across the flanks of Ecton Hill to reach the rim of the Manifold Valley with a sudden and spectacular view across this deep wooded valley. An exhilarating path then skirts across the top of this hillside before slanting steeply down across Ecton Hill to reach the hamlet of Ecton along the valley floor, with the scars of old mine workings scattered across the hillside. Copper has been mined on Ecton Hill since the Bronze Age, although the mines were at their most productive between the 17th and 19th Centuries. In the second half of the 18th Century they were amongst the richest in Europe and the Duke of Devonshire (who owned the mineral rights) became extremely wealthy from these mines, which helped finance improvements to Chatsworth House as well as the development of Buxton as a fashionable spa town. These old mines are incredibly deep with huge vertical shafts following the mineral veins over 1,000-ft below river level, drained by an ingenious system of underground water-powered pumps and drainage channels. The hamlet of Ecton lies sheltered along the valley floor, an attractive cluster of former mine buildings including the Mine Agent's House and Mine Office as well as an eccentric house with a green copper spire known as The Folly.

The course (and character) of the River Manifold roughly follows that of the River Dove until they join forces just downstream of Ilam. From its source near Flash, Britain's highest village, the river meanders through a broad valley hemmed in by undulating hills. Its character changes suddenly at Hulme End for here the river leaves the Dark Peak behind and races head first into the White Peak. Over aeons, the river has carved a dramatic gorge through this limestone plateau, which meanders in spectacular fashion through a fantastic landscape of thick woodland and towering limestone crags - 'manifold' means 'many folds'. This valley is threaded by the track-bed of the former Leek and Manifold Light Railway (LMLR), now the Manifold Way trail. The LMLR was a narrow-gauge branch railway that opened in 1904 to transport farm produce from this remote area to Leek and beyond. It ran for eight-and-a-half miles from its terminus at Hulme End at the northern tip of the Manifold Valley to Waterhouses where it connected with the standard gauge North Staffordshire Railway. The design of the locomotives and carriages were the same as a steam railway in India, with big headlamps on the front of the trains and verandas at the end of the carriages! The railway was a financial disaster as the builders had hoped that the Ecton Mines would re-open and the railway would be extended to Buxton, but neither happened and when the small creamery at Ecton closed in 1933 then it was the end of the line for the LMLR. Despite bringing thousands of tourists up to the Manifold Valley during summer weekends, the railway never made a profit and closed in 1934.

In the heart of the valley lies Wetton Mill, situated just across the low-slung stone packhorse bridge that was re-built in 1807 by the Duke of Devonshire following flood damage to keep this important route to his copper mines open. There has been a watermill here since medieval times, although the present building dates from the 18th Century. This corn mill last worked in the mid 19th Century, after which it became a farmhouse and is now a popular café. Further down the valley is the dramatic Thor's Cave set in a towering limestone rock-face high above the valley. The long climb up to this cave is worth the effort for the views across the valley are superb. Named after the Norse god Thor, the sloping cave mouth leads up into a large passageway that stretches back for some considerable distance. For the last 10,000 years, people and animals have used this cave for shelter. Excavations have revealed bones dating back to the end of the last Ice Age, although most of the finds date from the Neolithic and Bronze Ages including stone axes, pottery and jewellery thought to have been used as part of a burial. You too are using this cave for shelter, just like your ancestors did ten millennia ago!

# WETTON SUNDAY WALK

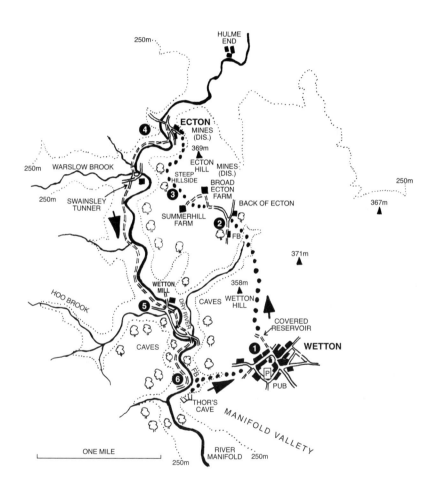

*1.* From the road junction in the centre of Wetton (with your back to
the Royal Oak) turn left up along the road towards 'Wetton Mill,
Butterton' then, where the road bends round to the left, take the
turning straight on to the right along a lane. Follow this metalled lane
bending up to the left (SP 'Back of Ecton'), climbing up out of the
village to reach a gate at the end of the metalled lane (small grass-
covered reservoir on your right). Head through the gate along the
track ahead then, where this track bends to the left after a short
distance, head through the squeeze-stile in the wall ahead. After this
stile, follow the path up the low bank to quickly reach a tumbledown
wall on your left, which you follow straight on (wall on your left) to
quickly reach another squeeze-stile (National Trust sign 'Wetton
Hill'). Cross the stile and walk straight on along the grassy path
across the hillside then drop down a short but steep bank to reach a
stile over a fence. Cross the stile then head to the right across the field
to reach another stile in the far corner. Cross the stile and follow the
path straight down the hillside alongside the wall on your left then,
where this wall bends away and the path forks, follow the right-hand
path straight on down across the grassy hillside to reach a small FB
across a stream/boggy ground in the far bottom corner of the field.
Cross the FB and head to the right over a stile, after which head
straight up the hillside bearing very slightly to the right to reach a
small gate that leads into woodland. After the gate, cross the
tumbledown wall just ahead then turn immediately right up through
sparse woodland to quickly join a road beside the entrance to a house.

*2.* Turn left up along the road to soon reach a T-junction where you turn
right and follow this road climbing steeply up. The road soon levels
out and bends round to the left before it drops gradually down then
bends sharply round to the right towards Broad Ecton Farm
(metalled lane becomes a stony track) - a few paces after this sharp
bend take the FP to the left over a wall-stile beside a gate (SP). After
the stile, head up across the field alongside the wall on your right
*(heading towards Summerhill Farm ahead)* then, halfway up the field,

head over a wall-stile beside a gate to your right (SP). After the wall-stile, follow the narrow path slanting up across the hillside, over a rutted farm track then carry on up to reach a large wall gap in the top corner of the field. After the wall gap, bear right across the field to reach a wall corner jutting out into the field - as you reach this wall corner, head to the left straight across the field to soon reach a wall-stile at the top of the steep wooded bank overlooking the Manifold Valley.

3. Cross the stile and follow the narrow path ahead to the right slanting across the steep hillside (houses of Swainsley far below) then, where this path forks after a short distance, follow the right-hand path straight on keeping to the same contour across the steep hillside to soon reach a promontory high above the Manifold Valley (overlooking Ecton). The path now curves slightly round to the right and heads across the steep hillside then, where the path forks, follow the left-hand path slanting down across the hillside passing below a spoil heap ringed by trees to reach a wall-stile hidden amongst trees at the bottom of the hillside beside a house. Cross the stile and turn right through an archway then follow the track straight on passing in front of the ornate house (copper spire) down passing cottages to join a road along the bottom of the valley. Turn right along the road then left after a short distance towards 'Warslow, Leek' then left again after a few paces along a metalled track, marked by a 'No Vehicles' sign (Manifold Way).

4. Follow this metalled track heading down the valley, over a bridge across the River Manifold then on through woodland to reach a road junction beside the long and narrow Swainsley Tunnel. Head through this old railway tunnel then follow the road meandering down through the Manifold Valley for 1.25 miles to reach a crossroads of lanes, with Wetton Mill just across the bridge to your left.

5. At this crossroads, head straight on along the lane ahead (SP 'Wetton, Alstonefield') and follow this heading down the valley (still walking along the former track-bed) running parallel with the valley road on your right, over a bridge across the (dry) River Manifold to soon reach a T-junction with this valley road, where you head straight

on through a gate and over a bridge across the dry riverbed ('No vehicles' sign). Carry straight on along the metalled track-bed (Manifold Way) meandering down through the valley for a further 0.5 miles then, where the track curves round to the right beneath Thor's Cave, turn left over a FB across the dry River Manifold.

6. Cross the FB and follow the path climbing up through woodland (stone steps) heading up out of the valley. *(Detour to Thor's Cave – after a short distance a path turns off to the right (SP 'Thor's Cave') climbing steeply up through woodland to reach Thor's Cave. Re-trace your steps back down to this path climbing up out of the valley).* Follow this path climbing steadily up through woodland (stone path ends after a while) to reach a small gate in a wall/fence at the top of the woods, after which carry straight on climbing up through a shallow grassy valley, through a gate in a wall then straight up across the (narrowing) field *(Wetton come into view ahead)* to reach a squeeze-stile through the wall to your left at the top of the field (SP). Turn right along the road back into Wetton.

*Wetton*

# YOULGRAVE

*What's in a name? It is pronounced Youlgrave, the road-sign into the village says Youlgrave yet the Ordnance Survey map and most guidebooks say Youlgreave. In fact, local historians have found over 50 variations of the name recorded throughout the centuries. The name is probably derived from 'yellow grove' as the word 'groove' is a local term for a lead mine – this was once an important centre for lead mining. Just to confuse matters even more, the village is known locally as Pommie! Noted for its narrow main street lined with old cottages and a clutch of traditional shops and inns, this linear village straddles a ridge of land between the limestone valleys of Lathkill Dale and Bradford Dale. Its focal point is the circular water storage tank known as the Fountain, built in 1829 to provide drinking water for the village piped from a spring near Mawstone Mine. Clean water was cause for great celebration, so much so that the villagers revived the ancient Well Dressing ceremony. Each June, the Fountain and five other old wells are 'dressed' with pictorial flower displays, some of the best in the Peak District. Overlooking Fountain Square is the former Co-Operative Stores, now used as a Youth Hostel, with its ornate Victorian frontage. All Saints Church dominates the village, its magnificent Perpendicular tower rising almost 100-ft above the rooftops. The present building dates back to the mid 12th Century, although it stands on a religious site used since Saxon times. The spacious nave is predominately Norman with lovely arcades and finely carved capitals, whilst the rest of the church dates from the 14th and 15th Centuries. Inside, look out for the tomb of a 13th Century knight and the 15th Century alabaster tomb of Thomas Cockayne dressed in armour who lived at nearby Harthill Hall.*

## THE VILLAGE

Youlgrave boasts three pubs, B&B's, Youth Hostel, general stores, delicatessen, butcher's shop, greengrocer, Post Office, telephone, toilets, bus service, garage and car park.

## ACCOMMODATION

Tourist Information Centre, Bakewell:     01629 816558

## YOULGRAVE PUBS

**Bull's Head Hotel, Youlgrave:**     **01629 636307**
This handsome old coaching inn stands in the heart of Youlgrave; note the coaching arch with a carved bull's head above. Inside, the original layout remains intact with a cosy bar complete with herringbone floor, separate snug, dining room and lounge warmed by an open fire.

**Farmyard Inn, Youlgrave:**     **01629 636221**
As the name suggests, this was originally a farmhouse although it has been a pub for almost 200 years. Inside, it is warm and welcoming with a narrow lounge complete with low beams and a large stone fireplace at the far end, whilst there is also a cosy tap room and separate upstairs dining room.

**George Hotel, Youlgrave:**     **01629 636292**
Overlooking All Saints Church with benches outside so you can watch the world go by and cars squeeze past each other along the narrow main street. Inside, this traditional pub retains its original layout with high ceilings and several rooms including a traditional bar, lounge and a 'corridor' drinking area.

## PUBS ALONG THE WALKS

Bull's Head, Monyash:               01629 812372
Druid Inn, Birchover:               01629 650302
Red Lion, Birchover:                01629 650363
Flying Childers, Stanton in Peak:   01629 636333

# Youlgrave Walking Weekend
## - Saturday Walk -
*Youlgrave, Lathkill Dale, Monyash, Cales Dale*
*& Bradford Dale*

## WALK INFORMATION

Highlights     Crystal clear waters, a tier of weirs, lead mining remains, ancient woodland, a profusion of wild flowers, marble quarries and the farm of naughty monks.

Distance     11.5 miles     Time    5 hours

Maps     OS Explorer OL24

Refreshments     Pubs and shops at Youlgrave. Pub and café at Monyash.

Terrain     Between Youlgrave and Monyash, this walk follows clear paths through Bradford Dale and Lathkill Dale alongside rivers, through woodland and across rough limestone terrain. From Monyash, field paths lead back towards Youlgrave, with a steep traverse of Cales Dale. There is quite a steep path down into Bradford Dale from where a riverside path leads through the valley back to Youlgrave.

Ascents     Low Moor Plantation - 310 metres above sea level.

Caution     Do not enter the old mine workings and caves through out Lathkill Dale and keep to the path at all times as there are hidden shafts. Some parts of Lathkill Dale are rough underfoot and may flood after heavy rain. Steep sections including Cales Dale and the descent into Bradford Dale. Limestone is slippery when wet.

NB:     The permissive path through Lathkill Dale National Nature Reserve (through Palmerston Wood) is closed on Wednesdays from October to January.

Bradford Dale is a secluded valley with steep slopes rising up to the houses of Youlgrave. A footpath traces the river down to its confluence with the River Lathkill at Alport, passing an old packhorse bridge along the way. Further upstream beyond the clapper bridge lie a series of small lakes known as Bradford Dams (which you will pass towards the end of this walk) teeming with fish and water fowl. Alport lies in a wooded hollow with running water all around, once the source of power for a corn mill in the heart of this village. Its name is derived from the Portway which crossed the river here, a prehistoric track-way that stretched north to south through the heart of the Peak District.

From Alport, a footpath follows the River Lathkill upstream across meadows to reach Conksbury Bridge which marks the beginning (or end) of arguably the finest limestone valley in England and the jewel in the crown of the Derbyshire Dales. At first, the valley is gentle and serene with a series of low weirs built to provide good trout fishing, but the true glory of Lathkill Dale lies beyond Lathkill Lodge. The stretch of valley between here and the old mill pond of Carter's mill above Palmerston Wood (whose foundations and mill-stones are still visible) forms part of the Derbyshire Dales National Nature Reserve with only a permissive path threading along the narrow valley floor. This path leads up through a truly wonderful landscape with a crystal clear river, said to be the purest in England, hemmed in by steep slopes cloaked in ash woodland. Lead has been mined in Lathkill Dale since at least the 13th Century, although mining was at its height during the 18th and 19th Centuries. Old workings abound, including the former Mandale Mine with its ruinous Engine House, levels, drainage sough and old pillars that once supported an aqueduct built to carry water to a waterwheel. Upstream of these old workings are the remains of the Lathkill Dale Mine known as Bateman's House. The Lathkill Dale Mining Company was established in 1825 by Thomas Bateman and John Alsop to tap into the deepest and richest part of the vein. They had to overcome severe flooding problems as the adjacent river flows over limestone, which is notoriously pervious. They employed James

Bateman as company agent who managed an ambitious scheme to dig a deep drainage shaft from where water was pumped out by a large 120-horsepower engine that was shielded by a house (now known as Bateman's House) where he and his family also lived. As the mines went deeper, more pumps were needed to keep the shafts dry but they could not keep the waters back and so the mine closed in 1842; in it heyday 120 miners were employed here. Steps lead down into this shaft from where you can see the main drainage shaft far below ground. Above Palmerston Wood, the character of the valley changes with sparse ash woodland, dramatic scree slopes and towering crags; note the small waterfall of Lathkill Falls where the river flows over a tufa dam. Beyond the side-valley of Cales Dale, the valley grows wilder and narrower. The path soon reaches the impressive opening of Lathkill Head Cave, the winter source of the river - *only experts should enter this dangerous cave.* Upper Lathkill Dale is renowned for its swathes of springtime flowers, as the steep limestone grassland provides the perfect habitat for orchids, cowslips and the very rare Jacob's ladder. The head of the valley is marked by a narrow cleft in the rocks, above which is Ricklow Quarry that once produced 'grey marble', a highly polished limestone that was used for fireplaces, staircases and other decorative items popular during the 18th and 19th Centuries.

Monyash is situated on the White Peak limestone plateau at the head of Lathkill Dale. It is a pleasant village of grey-stone cottages and farms grouped around an attractive green overlooked by a traditional pub. There is a 14th Century market cross on the green, a reminder of the days when this was a thriving trading centre at the heart of the Peak District lead mining industry. St Leonard's Church reflects the former importance of Monyash for it was founded in Norman times but extended and improved during the 14th Century with the addition of transepts, a wider nave, tower and imposing spire. As with many White Peak villages, it developed around several natural springs that at one time fed five ponds, although only Fere Mere remains. Nearby is One Ash Grange Farm, situated above the deep wooded cleft of Cales Dale, a tributary of Lathkill Dale. This former monastic farm once belonged to Roche Abbey and was where unruly monks were sent as punishment!

# YOULGRAVE SATURDAY WALK

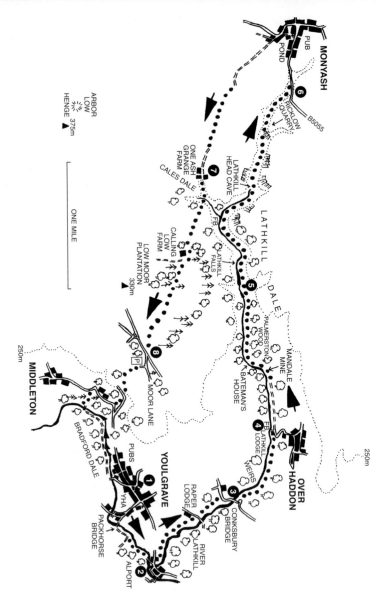

# THE WALK

1. From the Fountain in the centre of Youlgrave, turn left along the Main Street to reach All Saints Church. Turn right along the lane immediately before the church (Bradford Road leading to Mawstone Lane) and follow this quite steeply down then, just before the last house on your left (Braemar House), bear off to the left along an enclosed path passing behind Braemar House down to reach a packhorse bridge across the River Bradford. Cross the bridge and follow the wide gravel track to the left heading down through the valley (River Bradford to your left) then, where this track bends up to the right, head straight on through a kissing-gate. Follow the clear path straight on across a field (river just across to your left) to soon re-join the river again, which you follow downstream passing the limestone outcrop of Rhienstor to reach a gate across the track on the outskirts of Alport. Head through the gate, over a bridge across the river and straight on to join the main road beside a bridge across the River Lathkill.

2. At the road take the FP opposite through a wall-stile beside a gate (SP 'Conksbury') and follow the path straight on across the field (ignore track behind the buildings) to reach a small gate in the far corner. A clear path now heads straight on alongside a wall on your right across several fields and through a series of squeeze-stiles (with the River Lathkill just across to your right) for just over 0.5 miles to reach a narrow road just below Raper Lodge. At the road, carry straight on along the rough track opposite (SP 'Lathkill Dale') and follow this straight on with woodland on your right then, where this woodland ends and the track bends to the right into a field, head straight on through a small gate in a fence. Follow the path ahead to reach a road where you turn right down to reach Conksbury Bridge across the River Lathkill.

3. Cross Conksbury Bridge, a short distance after which take the turning to the left (SP) through a gate and follow the wide path down through woodland to join the banks of the River Lathkill.

Carry straight on along this clear path heading up through the valley (river to your left) passing a series of weirs and small lakes. After 0.5 miles the path becomes slightly rougher underfoot as it crosses limestone and leads on through the wooded valley *(river now follows a natural course rather than artificial lakes)* to reach a clapper bridge and ford across the river beside Lathkill Lodge.

4. Turn right up along the lane for a few paces then turn left along a stony track skirting around the old mill building to reach a gate on the edge of the National Nature Reserve *(permissive path through the Nature Reserve).* Head through the gate and follow the track straight on heading up through wooded Lathkill Dale, with the river to your left. After just under 0.5 miles you pass between two old stone gateposts and enter woodland, with the Mandale Mine drainage sough beside the track to your left *(Mandale Mine Engine House just up to your right in the woodland).* Continue straight on along the wide track through the woodland (river still on your left) passing the stone-built supports of the old aqueduct, after which carry on along the clear track heading up through the wooded valley to soon reach a FB across the river that leads to Bateman's House (lead mine ruins). After visiting the ruins, continue along the clear track heading up through Palmerston Wood with the River Lathkill on your left for about 0.75 miles to reach a gate at the end of Palmerston Wood/Nature Reserve.

5. Head through the gate and walk straight on to quickly reach another gate (track ends), after which follow the riverside path straight on *(Carter's mill pond on your left)* heading up through steep-sided Lathkill Dale passing Lathkill Falls (path becomes rougher underfoot) and on through sparse woodland to soon reach a wall-stile across your path. Cross the stile and follow the stony path heading up through the valley along the wooded riverbank for about 0.5 miles to reach a crossroads of paths beside a FB (valley opens out - woodland left behind). Do not cross this FB but continue along the narrow path alongside the river on your left heading up along the valley floor. You soon pass the summer source of the river, beyond which the riverbed is often dry - continue along the narrow path heading up through the

valley alongside a wall on your left following the valley as it gently curves round to the left. Where the wall ends with Lathkill Head Cave just to your left (winter source of the river) carry on along the narrow path heading up through the dry limestone valley to reach a wall-stile towards the head of the valley. Cross the stile and follow the rough path up over boulders through a narrow limestone valley - the valley soon opens out and you come to a kissing-gate across your path at the head of Lathkill Dale. Head through the kissing-gate and follow the broad grassy path up through the shallow valley to reach the B5055 on the outskirts of Monyash.

6. Turn left up along the road into Monyash to reach the green in the centre of the village. As you reach the top of the green, turn left at the crossroads towards 'Newhaven, Youlgreave' along Rakes Road and follow this through the village passing Fere Mere on your left then, where the road bends sharply to the right at the top of the village, carry straight on along a track (SP 'Limestone Way'). Where this track forks after a short distance, follow the left-hand walled track straight on leaving Monyash behind. Follow this track for just over 0.5 miles (track becomes an enclosed path) to reach a small gate at the end of the walled path, after which head straight on alongside the wall on your right for about 50 yards then cross the wall-stile to the right (SP). After the wall-stile, head left across the field to reach a squeeze-stile in a wall (SP), after which head up alongside the wall on your left across two fields then, as you approach the end of the second field, cross the wall-stile to the left just before a gate in the field corner (SP). After this wall-stile, turn right alongside the wall on your right and follow this down to reach a gate in the bottom field corner that leads onto a track which you follow down to reach One Ash Grange Farm.

7. As you reach the farmhouse, follow the track to the left (waymarkers) skirting behind the farmhouse then, where the track forks just beyond the farmhouse, follow the right-hand track down towards the farm buildings and walk between a Dutch barn and a stone barn to reach a stile that leads down steps out onto a field. Head straight on to reach a bridle-gate at the top of Cales Dale.

Head through the gate and follow the path down through a rocky cleft then head straight on beneath a limestone rock-face on your left for about 100 yards then turn right (SP) steeply down to reach a stile over a fence in the valley bottom. Cross the stile and follow the path climbing steeply up stone steps out of the valley to reach a kissing-gate at the top of the climb. Head through the gate and walk straight up across the field to a kissing-gate, after which continue up across the next field to another kissing-gate (beside a larger gate) in the top field corner. Head through this gate and bear right across the field to reach a kissing-gate beside a larger gate (barns across to your right), after which turn left to reach a gate that leads into woodland. Head through the narrow belt of woodland and through another kissing-gate after which head straight on across the field bearing slightly to the right (Calling Low Farm across to your right) and through a bridle-gate in a wall. Follow the path through woodland to quickly reach a kissing-gate that leads out onto a field. After this kissing-gate, turn right down across the field to reach another kissing-gate, after which head diagonally to the left across the field to reach a gate/stile in the far corner that leads into Low Moor Plantation. Follow the path keeping close to the wall on your left to quickly reach a bridle-gate at the end of the woods, after which head straight on across the field to reach a stile over a fence. Cross the stile and continue straight on bearing slightly to the right across the large field down to reach a wall-stile at the bottom of the field, after which head left over another wall-stile and then walk straight on to reach a squeeze-stile in the field corner that leads onto the road near a road junction.

8. Turn left along the road for a few paces then take the right fork (Moor Lane) and follow this down for about 200 yards to reach Moor Lane Car Park. Take the track to the right immediately after the car park (SP) and follow this wide path straight on (ignore the fork to the right towards the small barn) to reach a small wall-gate. Head through the wall-gate and walk straight on down across the field then, halfway across the field, follow the path bending round to the left (passing the end of a tumbledown wall) then heading

steadily down across the hillside to join a road. Turn left along the road for a short distance then take the FP to the right (SP) and follow the path straight down across the field to join another road. Turn right along the road passing the entrance to Lomberdale Hall then, where the road drops down and bends sharply round to the left, take the FP to the left (immediately after the sharp bend) through a squeeze-stile in the wall (beside a stone seat in wall). Follow the path down through woodland with a ravine to your left at first then winding down to reach a bridge across the River Bradford. Cross the bridge and turn left along the wide path heading down through Bradford Dale passing a series of small lakes (Bradford Dams) for about 0.75 miles to reach a clapper bridge beside a ford across the river. Cross this bridge and follow the lane steeply back up into Youlgrave.

# Youlgrave Walking Weekend
## - Sunday Walk -
### *Youlgrave, Robin Hood's Stride, Nine Ladies Stone Circle & Stanton in Peak*

## WALK INFORMATION

Highlights
: Mystical moorlands, stone circles and a hermit's cave, a Druid's temple, Bronze Age burial grounds, expansive views, hillside villages and a classic Peakland pub.

Distance
: 8 miles    Time    4 hours

Maps
: OS Explorer OL24

Refreshments
: Pubs and shops at Youlgrave and Birchover. Pub at Stanton in Peak.

Terrain
: Field paths (muddy in places) lead up across Harthill Moor to join the B5056, which is followed for a short distance before a muddy path and then a track lead up into Birchover. After a short section of road-walking, a wide path heads across Stanton Moor to reach Nine Ladies Stone Circle set in a clearing (confusing maze of paths). The wide path continues through woodland to join a lane that leads down into Stanton in Peak. This road is followed down through the village to join the B5056, from where field and riverside paths as well as quiet country lanes lead back to Youlgrave.

Ascents
: Stanton Moor - 307 metres above sea level.

Caution
: Take care exploring Robin Hood's Stride, Cratcliff Tor and Rowter Rocks - sheer drops and hidden crevices. Take care when walking along roads around Stanton in Peak.

# POINTS OF INTEREST

The whole swathe of land between Youlgrave and Birchover is a mystical landscape littered with relics from a forgotten age. There is an atmosphere that hangs heavy in the air, a feeling that you are amongst something very special and very old; a feeling that you are not alone. The Portway, that ancient Iron Age route which linked important cultural and spiritual sites throughout the Peak District, cuts across Harthill Moor passing the Iron Age hill-fort of Castle Ring and the Bronze Age Nine Stones stone circle, although only four remain standing. Were these stones in alignment with the rock formations of Robin Hood's Stride? This large outcrop of gritstone rocks dominates Harthill Moor, indeed, it is sometimes known as Mock Beggar Hall due to its turreted appearance when viewed from a distance silhouetted against the skyline. Just to the east hidden amongst trees at the foot of Cratcliff Tor is the Hermit's Cave. This small cave was certainly occupied by a hermit during the 16th Century as it is mentioned in the records of Haddon Hall. He would have preached to travellers along the Portway. Historians believe that this cave is much older and that the carving of Jesus and the lamp recess are actually 700 years old.

The grey-stone houses of Birchover are situated on a hillside just below Stanton Moor. Again, it is the rocks that bring people to Birchover. Behind the Druid Inn stand the Rowtor Rocks, a wonderful collection of gritstone outcrops carved and fashioned into fantastic shapes by nature and man. A maze of steps, caves, passageways, seats, rooms and a three-seater armchair have been carved out of solid rock. According to local legend, these rock cuttings were made by Druids thousands of years ago as a temple and sacrificial altar, although they were most probably made by the local vicar Thomas Eyre in the early 18th Century when he built an eccentric study for himself! Truth and myth are closely intertwined for there are several prehistoric carvings (including cup and ring marked rocks) across the outcrops, which adds weight to the theory that this was a pagan site. The Reverend Eyre also built a chapel along the lane just down from the Druid Inn in about 1700.

Above Birchover lies Stanton Moor, a magical swathe of moorland carpeted with heather and dotted with birch woodland, an outpost of the Dark Peak set amidst the eastern edges of the White Peak. This is one of the most important Bronze Age sites in England with over seventy cysts and burial mounds, numerous standing stones and stone circles. The finest of these is the Nine Ladies Stone Circle, set in clearing above the steep escarpment overlooking the Derwent Valley. This stone circle was built around 4,000 years ago and was originally surrounded by an earthen bank. Its purpose remains unknown, although rituals and ceremonies certainly took place here, probably associated with the solstices. It is a very atmospheric place, especially in the depths of winter when the low sun slants through the trees. According to legend, the Nine Ladies were turned to stone for dancing on the Sabbath, whilst the King Stone was the fiddler - the King Stone is situated about 40 yards to the west. Such stories have often been attributed to stone circles as a way of Christianising a pagan site, thus trivialising Bronze Age culture. During the early 20th Century father and son team J.C. and J.P. Heathcote of Birchover excavated many of the burial mounds and displayed their finds in a small museum they set up, later moved to the Sheffield Weston Park Museum. Nearby is the Earl Grey Tower, built in 1832 to commemorate the passing of the Reform Bill.

Stanton in Peak is a delightful hillside village situated on the north-western flanks of Stanton Moor with stone houses, a lovely church and great country pub lining the sloping main street. This is essentially an estate village of Stanton Hall, home of the Thornhill family, who rebuilt much of the village during the 19th Century - look out for the initials WPT. At the heart of the village is the Flying Childers pub, named after a famous winning racehorse that belonged to the Duke of Devonshire during the 18th Century. This unspoilt Peakland pub boasts a traditional bar complete with wooden settles, beamed ceiling and a coal fire. Opposite the pub stands Holly House, a fine three-storey early Georgian house that still has two blocked-up windows, a result of the 1697 Windows Tax, although until recently a further six windows were also blocked up.

*For more information about Alport, see Saturday Walk*

# YOULGRAVE SUNDAY WALK

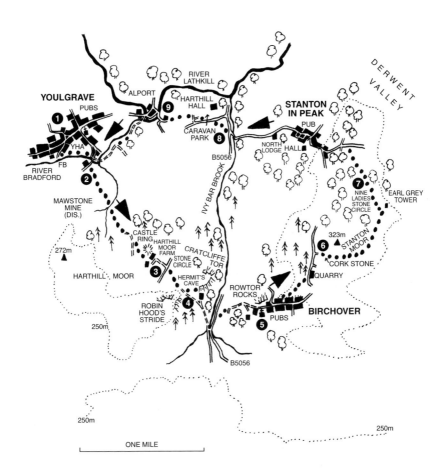

213

# THE WALK

*1.* From the circular stone Fountain in the centre of Youlgrave, turn right along the Main Street (away from the church) then left along Holywell Lane (by the 'phone box) passing the Wesleyan Reform Chapel on your left. Follow this lane steeply down out of the village to reach an old clapper bridge/ford across the River Bradford. Turn left through a gate immediately before the clapper bridge (SP) and follow the riverside path heading down the valley, passing a series of small dams, to soon reach a road beside a cluster of houses at the bottom end of Youlgrave. Turn right along the road over the bridge across the River Bradford then, after 150 yards (just before the 'National Speed Limit' signs), take the first FP to the left through a squeeze-stile (SP).

*2.* After the squeeze-stile, bear slightly right across the field through another squeeze-stile after which turn immediately left alongside the wall on your left then, as you approach the bottom corner of the field bear slightly right through a squeeze-stile beside a gate. After the squeeze-stile, follow the muddy track straight on up through another gate, after which carry on alongside the wall on your left through another gate in the field corner. After this third gate, head to the right across the middle of the field passing a telegraph pole and down over a small wooded stream and a stile just beyond. After the stile, head straight up across the field bearing very slightly to the right and cross over an overgrown hedge-line at the top of this first field, after which bear left up across the middle of the field to reach some old stone gateposts (on their own) at the foot of a steep grassy bank. A muddy track now leads to the left gradually rising up across this bank then levelling out and bending round to the right to reach a gate just down to your left in an overgrown hedge at the bottom of a small valley *(Castle Ring hill-fort up ahead)*. After the gate, follow the narrow path heading quite steeply up to the right across the steep hillside (marker-posts) passing just below the hill-fort to reach a large wall gap in the top field corner (barns of Harthill Moor Farm ahead).

Head through the wall gap and follow the track straight on to quickly reach a stile over a fence just to the left of the large barns (farmhouse across to your left). Cross the stile then walk on to join the farm lane which you follow to the left then bending sharp right away from the farmhouse to reach a road.

3. At the road take the FP opposite through a gate (SP) and head to the right across the field *(Robin Hood's Stride ahead)* to reach a wall-stile just to the left of a gate *(Nine Stones stone circle across to your left in the next field)*. After the wall-stile head diagonally to the left up across the middle of the field to reach a stile beside a gate in the far corner of the field just below the outcrops of Robin Hood's Stride. After the gate, turn immediately left over a stile across a fence that leads onto a rough track (The Portway). Turn right down along the rough track then, after a short distance, cross the wall-stile to your left, marked by a SP *(detour to the Hermit's Cave)*. After the wall-stile, follow the path keeping close to the fence/woodland on your right climbing up at first then straight on to reach a wall-stile that leads out onto an area of outcrops and woodland (Cratcliff Tor). After the wall-stile pick your way between the boulders and trees to the right dropping down then skirting just below the boulders through trees to quickly reach the Hermit's Cave. *Re-trace your steps back to the rough track near Robin Hood's Stride (The Portway).*

4. At the rough track, head down to the left along the track, through a gate and out onto a field where you carry on down alongside the wall on your right to join the clear stony lane leading from Cratcliff Cottage. Follow this lane down to the right to reach a lane beside its junction with the main road. Turn left to quickly reach the main road then left again along the main road *(take care)* for about 200 yards then, where the road begins to gently curve left, take the FP to the right over a stile (SP 'Birchover'). Follow the grassy path bearing to the left heading up across the hillside to reach a stile beside a bridlegate (just below the top of the wooded hill) that leads onto a clear track. Turn left along this track and follow it skirting around the wooded hill to join a clearer track on a sharp bend - follow the left-

hand track straight on. The track becomes a walled lane that leads up passing the Old Vicarage to join the Main Street through Birchover beside the Druid Inn.

5. Turn right along the Main Street then take the enclosed FP to the left immediately after the Red Lion Inn. Follow this up skirting to the left of a house passing behind the Red Lion Inn then up a steep bank to reach a wide path. Turn right and follow this path up through woodland to reach the quarry car park and the road just beyond. Turn left along the road passing the quarry buildings and then a quarry road on your right, after which continue on for a further 200 yards then turn right along the clear FP (SP), up over a stile that leads out onto the heather moorland of Stanton Moor. Head straight on to quickly reach the grit-stone outcrop of the Cork Stone, complete with hand-grips.

6. Where the path forks beside the Cork Stone, follow the right-hand path straight on across the heather moorland (keep to the clear wide path) to reach a crossroads of clear paths after 400 yards. Carry straight on along the wide path heading across the heather moorland to soon join a grassy path coming in from your right. Follow this path to the left all the way to reach a fork in the path just before you enter the sparse birch woodland (Earl Grey Tower just ahead). Follow the left-hand path through the sparse woodland (Tower just across to your right) then follow the path bearing to the left to quickly reach Nine Ladies stone circle set in a clearing.

7. As you reach the stone circle (beside the Information Board) you come to a clear, wide path across your path which you follow to the right through the trees (ignore any paths off this main path) to soon join a fence/wall on your right along the edge of the woodland. Follow this straight on along the edge of the woodland to soon reach a stile beside a gate across your path. Cross the stile then carry straight on along the clear path along the woodland edge to reach another gate that leaves the woodland and Stanton Moor behind. Follow the grassy path straight on across two fields to reach a gate that leads onto a road. Turn left along the road (ignore quarry track)

and follow this down into Stanton in Peak. At the road junction in the village, turn right towards 'Pilhough, Bakewell' down through the village centre passing Holy Trinity Church and then the Flying Childers pub. Continue along this road down out of the village *(take care)* dropping steadily down passing North Lodge (high estate wall on your left) before a final steep bend down to the right to reach the main road.

8. At the road take the FP opposite (SP) over a wall-stile, after which head to the right up alongside the fence/wall on your right for a short distance then, where this bends to the right, pass through an old squeeze-stile then head left up across the middle of the field passing to the left of a small barn to reach a gate in the top far corner that leads onto a lane (SP). Turn left along the lane and follow this gently curving round to the left for about 200 yards then take the FP to the right (SP) over a stile through the hedge. Follow the path through a belt of trees and out onto a caravan park - head straight on to quickly join the track through the caravan park where you head left to quickly reach a T-junction with another track. At this T-junction, take the FP opposite to the right alongside a wooden fence to quickly reach a squeeze-stile, after which bear right across the field through another squeeze-stile in the bottom corner then head straight on along the bottom edge of two more fields (caravan site) through squeeze-stiles to join an enclosed path. Follow this path straight on down to reach a road on a sharp bend beside a house. Turn right steeply down the road to reach the bridge across the River Lathkill at Alport.

9. Cross the bridge then turn immediately left along the road through the village and up to reach the main road where you turn left over another bridge across the River Lathkill immediately after which turn left beside the 'phone box along a driveway (SP). Follow this driveway straight on passing some houses to your right then, where the driveway forks, head straight on over a bridge across the River Bradford and through a white gate. Follow this track straight on with the river to your right to reach a kissing-gate that leads onto a clear driveway. Follow this to the right (river still to your right), passing an

old packhorse bridge and then some limestone outcrops (keep to clear driveway) all the way to re-join the road beside the bridge across the River Bradford at the bottom end of Youlgrave. Head straight on with the river on your left (and cottages on your right) through the gate ahead that leads onto the riverside path - re-trace your steps straight on with the river on your left back to reach the clapper bridge where you turn right up along Holywell Lane back up into Youlgrave.

*Youlgrave*

Top: Hope Cross

Middle: Eyam Church

Bottom: Kinder Reservoir

© Mark Reid

*Top: Parkhouse Hill*

*Middle: Froggatt Edge*

*Bottom: Lode Mill*

© *Mark Reid*

*Top: The Great Ridge*
*Middle: North Lees Hall*
*Bottom: Thor's Cave*
*© Mark Reid*

Top:
*Win Hill (from Lose Hill)*

Middle:
*The Quiet Woman*

Bottom:
*Cave Dale*

© Mark Reid